BECOMING LIKE JESUS

How To Think and Live Like Jesus Christ

John Avery

CONTENTS

THE SPARKS SERIES

The pieces I write are not exactly devotionals though they have some of the flavor of a devotional: they are short enough to be read in a few minutes and can be used daily for a few weeks, each is a reflection on at least one Bible verse, and some life application is encouraged. However, the pieces are designed to stimulate deeper reflection than many contemporary devotionals. I think of these pieces as sparks.

Jesus' life and words frequently challenged people's established ways of living. He didn't come to bless life as we know it; He invites us to lay down our old ways and receive His kingdom life instead. When a wildfire rages through brush, it quickly consumes the dead and the dry. After the rain, and the space of a few weeks, new life sprouts. I pray that these pieces will be sparks to lives that are surrendered to burning and committed to the slower process of nurturing kingdom ways in place of the old.

My prayer is that a flame would ignite in your brain, fire up your thinking, race to your heart, and jump from the tips of your fingers, toes, and tongue. Feed the flames so that your thoughts turn to passion, and your passion to action. May it be of such intensity that, everywhere you walk, every life that you touch begins to glow in turn.

No fire has value except the fire of the glory of God. The words of the Bible are more important than mine. For the sake of space, I have included only a few verses in each piece (noted on the Contents page). So, please take time to reflect on each Scripture in its context and, if possible, read any parallel accounts (provided under chapter headings). Imagine the scenes and consider the characters. As I reflected on the passages, the Spirit's finger pointed at things in my life and inspired each piece; ask Him to work in your life too. It's His finger that beckons us out of our old ways and points us to the ways of Jesus.

May you burn with His fire as a result of contemplating these simple sparks.

Look out for other compilations of short pieces in titles or on topics like:

The Questions of Jesus Published October 2022
The Kingdom of God Published March 2023
Our Identity as Children of God
Conversation with God (commonly called prayer)
Faith in God
The Spirit of God
Following the Voice of God (calling and guidance)
Revival from God
Prophets of God
Names of God
Followers of Jesus (what it means to be a disciple)
Kings of Israel (David, Saul, and others)
Fathers of Faith (Abraham, Jacob, and Moses)

Introduction to Becoming Like Jesus

"John, do you think Jesus and His disciples would have signed autographs?" Larry Norman's response to my request poured iced water on my thrill at meeting him. He was headlining a Christian rock festival, and I had a backstage pass—a splendid advantage for a budding autograph collector. Once I had recovered, I realized that the answer Larry implied by strolling away had ended my brief foray into that hobby. It was the first time I had seriously grappled with what it means to live like Jesus. It forced me to take the issue seriously even in a relatively trivial activity.

My struggle with the question started superficially in Sunday school when I was eight years old. From outside appearances, Jesus was a bearded flannelgraph figure in white who said and did good things. Was I supposed to dress His way—sandals and all? Take up carpentry like Him? Should I learn to talk like Him? How could I perform those signs and wonders? His teachings and miracles weren't part of the life I saw around me. I didn't notice people at church looking or talking much like Jesus, either. Failing my woodworking class at high school was a big setback. The disconnect went on for decades.

The glowing halo that Jesus wears in some artwork represents another problem. Jesus did and said special things because He was holy, right? But I'm a sinner, right? That was the gist of it. Being like Jesus seemed like an unreachable goal.

I understood better only when I dug below the surface of the beard and sandaled feet covered with dust. Forget the sandals, the beard, and especially the halo; being *like* Him means sharing a big part of His worldview, character, and action. He was unique and worth imitating because of His fundamentally different perspective, which centered on being God's Son. He was so clear about His identity that the knowledge touched His entire life. Likewise, for us to become like Jesus, we must start from the inside and work outwards.

Now, I am no expert imitator; I'm on the same journey as you. The pieces I share here were inspired by years of reflection on Jesus. I have long asked in what ways He is different. How different? And the vital question—the extent to which we can imitate Him. I have tried to filter out two things: aspects of our individual personalities that will and should always remain, and Jesus' pure divinity, which we can never share. What's left are ways in which we can be like Him.

As you reflect on these pieces, ask yourself two questions. What would you do in situations like the ones Jesus encountered? What was it about Jesus' way of thinking that enabled Him to live so differently? Then, of course, we should decide how to change our ways to be like Him. Actually, this book is not primarily about *how* to be like Jesus; it's not "how to be Christlike in five easy steps." Rather, it's about *who* He is. But don't miss a key point—contemplating and copying the inner life of the *Who* is the *how*.

Perhaps it's common to think that the price of becoming like Jesus is too high. Won't people we are close to find us strange, fanatical, aloof, judgmental, even offensive? Some of that concern comes from misunderstanding Jesus. We find no sign of most of those characteristics in Jesus, although religious leaders were offended by Him. A large part of learning to imitate Jesus is learning to love as He did, which may include fine-tuning the delivery of hard truths and warnings. Learning from Him will overturn any simplistic ideas about love.

What about our kids and our friends? Do we really want them to be like Jesus or would we rather enjoy them just as they are right now? Would Christlike kids make us proud or uncomfortable?

If we're honest, when it comes to being like Jesus, some of us set a limit, while others feel unable to grow beyond a certain point. What those barriers are and where they lie varies, but at some point, we decide that we won't imitate Him any more than we already have—that newly-revealed aspect of His life seems undesirable, unattainable, or simply unnecessary for our Christlikeness. As you read, be frank about your perceived barriers to growth. These pieces can help you identify them and pursue the path to greater maturity.

Anyway, why does it matter how Christlike we are? Most people probably focus on being a nice person or a good Christian without considering what Jesus would mean by "Christian," if He ever used the word (which He didn't). For most, being Christlike amounts to being a good churchgoer: attending, serving, fellowshipping, giving, and practicing what the leaders teach. Now, I'm not being cynical, but the Bible tells us in different ways to *be like Jesus* (Gal. 4:19; Phil. 2:5; 3:15). Our best leaders will tell us to imitate *Him*, not them (1 Cor. 11:1; Eph. 5:1). Another reason to imitate Him is that Jesus' accomplishments fit into a few grand themes, some of which He modeled for us to copy. Don't you think it's likely that being like Jesus in the way we listen to God, dodge the world's distractions, resist Satan, and make disciples will make us more fruitful in His kingdom work? I am convinced that we will escape from the impotence and irrelevance of superficial religion only to the extent that we make Christlikeness our goal.

THE MAN-GOD

The nature of Jesus is expressed well in the Sanskrit word, *Narahari,* meaning "man-God.[1]" Think about this—Jesus was God in human flesh, which also means that Jesus lived a human life full of God. Sometimes we see examples of both together: when He walked across the lake but climbed into the boat (instead of levitating), or when the risen Jesus entered the room with locked doors but ate a piece of fish. At other times, He appears distinctly human (His anguish in Gethsemane) or impressively divine (His transfiguration).

Our creeds rightly state Jesus was fully God and fully man. But the latter takes some thought given that all humans are fallen. Jesus shared humanness but not fallenness. In that sense, He's a different kind of human, with all the potential to fall but the will to stand firm. He shared the human soft spots that temptation targets—our every appetite, a central self, and vulnerabilities screaming for defenses. But He chose to believe what His divinity made clear, resisted temptation, and lived the glorious human existence that the rest of us have fallen from (John 1:14). So, Jesus did two basic things: He showed us what God is like clothed in human flesh and living a human life, and He showed us what we can aspire to when the Spirit of God completely fills us.

This is important because humans were made in the image of God. We share a measure of the nature of God. Jesus *"is the image of the invisible God"* (Col. 1:15); He demonstrated what we can be like if we allow God's life to fill us and only the most basic limitations to remain. The only limitations on God in Jesus involved

---

1. For a more complete explanation of its use as a title for Christ, see the CD *Amrit Vani* by Aradhna, 2007.

space, time, and energy. Jesus could be in only one place at one time, with just so much energy, and He had a limited lifespan.

For sure, those are significant restrictions, but consider how free Jesus was from the things that keep us from the abundant relationships that Jesus enjoyed with the Father and other people. Jesus experienced life without *needing* people, provision, or purpose; God met His needs. He could withdraw from others in a healthy way, without rejecting them or being aloof or self-indulgent. Neither peer pressure nor persecution swayed Him. Jesus had no ego to stroke—He glorified His Father. He came with no childhood wounds to lick. His communication with God wasn't distorted, so He had no doubts. And He pursued no idols or wrong agendas. Temptation never conquered Him because He shared the values of the Father; obedience to Him meant everything to Jesus.

While you ask God to fill you with more of His Spirit, ask Him to reduce your particular plague of unnecessary limitations. Ask Him to increase your confidence in Him as the Father who meets all your needs. Learn a healthy approach to relationships—loving others with no need to be loved back or to control them. Allow Him to expose and evict your idols. Have Him teach you what it means to seek His glory above everything else. The key to all this is an unobstructed relationship with the Father.

THE BONDSERVANT

Have this attitude in yourselves which was also in Christ Jesus, who, although He existed in the form of God, did not regard equality with God a thing to be grasped, but emptied Himself, taking the form of a bondservant, and being made in the likeness of men. And being found in appearance as a man, He humbled Himself by becoming obedient to the point of death, even death on a cross. Therefore also God highly exalted Him, and bestowed on Him the name which is above every name, that at the name of Jesus every knee should bow, of those who are in heaven, and on earth, and under the earth, and that every tongue should confess that Jesus Christ is Lord, to the glory of God the Father. (Philippians 2:5–11)

As a biologist, I learned about the life cycles of various creatures. You know, Adult—Egg—Larva—Pupa—Adult, and then more eggs. Paul tells us of a progression that Jesus went through, although it's not a repeating cycle.

From eternity, Jesus shared God's form and was equal with Him. To fulfill the purpose of God, He emptied Himself of many divine privileges and became a serving human—serving His Father. The strength of His serving heart and the depth of His humility were tested and proven by the distractions and opposition He had to endure from people and Satan. Ultimately, He obediently laid down His life (Heb. 5:8). The greatest miracle followed—His resurrection. The Father honored His obedience with exaltation and the name above all others.

It isn't natural to have Jesus' attitude, is it? From childhood, we prefer to be served. Parents and other influencers encourage us to make a name for ourselves, to become "something." The paths we take are manifold; most aim "high," few head "downwards." There's nothing wrong with developing and using natural abilities and becoming successful, even famous. The point is, do we share Jesus' attitude of obedient, humble service?

We start rather like Jesus in verse five—empty humans, but made in God's image, though we are fallen. That is our baseline identity. From that beginning, we make a choice: Jesus' way or a path we blaze on our own. On our quest for greatness, we reject emptiness, strive for and accomplish some temporary illusion of fullness, but end empty. Accepting our emptiness and the validity of Jesus' path to fullness is the only alternative to such vanity. Jesus redefined greatness as service and sacrifice (Matt. 20:25–28).

Jesus' first recorded words were spoken in the temple, "Did you not know that I had to be about My Father's business?" (Luke 2:49). At twelve years old, that was already His priority. Serving someone depends on understanding that person, listening to detailed instructions, and knowing their desires. Jesus listened to His Father, attended to what He was doing, and so ministered in His wisdom, love, and power. Imitating Jesus begins with focusing on who God is instead of what we can become.

One of the tests of a bondservant is waiting. After the incident in the temple, Jesus spent His teenage years submitted to His family and learning a trade. He seemed so ordinary that locals struggled to accept Him when He began His ministry. True bondservants can wait for their assignments. Their submission is more important than completed tasks.

But how do we balance submission to God and submission to human leaders? Serving human leaders and organizations is healthy; often it's taught and expected as part of personal development. But be careful—Jesus was God's servant first. Human masters sometimes obscure our service to God by asking us to help them build their little empires. True bond service involves listening to the Father and obeying Him. Only when a human leader is aligned with the Father's will and ways does assisting them and promoting their goals amount to serving the Father.[1]

---

1. Even people with no relationship with God can share some of His attributes like justice, compassion, generosity, peacemaking, etc.

Testing Times

(Context: Matthew 3:13–4:11. Parallels: Mark 1:9–13; Luke 3:21–22; 4:1–13; John 1:29–34.)

Jesus was still dripping wet from baptism when the Holy Spirit alighted and the Father spoke.[1]

Behold, a voice out of the heavens, saying, "This is My beloved Son, in whom I am well-pleased." Then Jesus was led up by the Spirit into the wilderness to be tempted by the devil. (Matthew 3:17–4:1)

Now, why would the Spirit lead Him from that experience into a harsh wilderness to be tested by the Tester?[2] At first glance, it seems strange for the Father to do this to His beloved Son. When God lays a foundation in our lives in the form of a miraculous sign or a word of promise or prophecy, the idea is for us to march ahead with faith. However, faith must be durable enough to enable us to fulfill God's plans. Testing times do more than prove faith, they strengthen it too. Tested faith is the basis for action and further faith.

Jesus faced tests from three angles. Two were directed straight at His sonship. "If you are the Son of God," use your power to feed yourself. "If you are . . ."

---

1. Luke 4:1 says the Spirit filled Him too.

2. "Tempter" (Matt. 4:3) is an unhelpful translation, all the words for testing or tempting in this passage and the parallels are translations of *peirasmos*.

contested His identity. Second, "Show that the Father cares for you, His Son, by jumping off a tall building." In that test, Satan suggested a kind of magic-thinking about a Scripture promise (Ps. 91:11–12). The third was an attempt to divert Jesus. Satan offered a shortcut to authority and glory, but in the world's way, not God's way. It tested Jesus' sonship differently.

Jesus' instant responses drew from Scripture. Here, and throughout His life, God's word formed the foundation of His faith. He never added to, subtracted from, multiplied, or divided it. His approach to Scripture was central to who He was—an example for all of us.

Satan's strategic tests of Jesus' sonship point to two other things we can learn:

1. The object and foundations of our faith should not be tested except by what arises from walking in the light of them—life brings its own tests. Jesus did not need to prove His sonship, and He told Satan that God must not be tested. Jesus was secure in the truth of His relationship with the Father, ready to live it out. May we grow in the assurance of our identity too. Like Jesus, to be fully committed, we must be totally convinced.

2. The essence of sonship is to be filled and led by the Spirit of the Father into a partnership with the Father. The Spirit led and empowered Jesus (Luke 4:14) while He learned obedience through what He suffered (Phil. 2:8; Heb. 5:8). Suffering measured the value Jesus put on obedience to the Father, the price He was willing to pay. He paid top dollar. Many junctions on life's path offer us the choice to live as a child who pleases the Father, or not. The Tester suggests an easier route to a nicer destination at each one. This third test of suggested shortcuts is ongoing. There are no shortcuts to His purposes, and the world's glory is worthless.

Spiritual Maturity—Nothing to Brag About

(Context: Ephesians 4:1–16.)

Perhaps it's because I'm a guy, but something in me wants to be the best: the top of the class, the fastest runner, the tallest, the winner of every game, the most spiritually mature, and the humblest. It took me years to realize that the ambitions for spiritual maturity and humility are often the greatest handicaps.

So what is spiritual maturity, and can we ever achieve it? A few disciplines have traditionally been associated with spiritual stature. Embracing those lifestyles could well help one to grow in maturity, but the practices are not essential and do not represent the essence of spiritual maturity.

- A perennial favorite is solitude. The monastic lifestyle certainly has helped people to focus on spiritual things, but unless we apply our contemplative insights to everyday life, seclusion does not develop maturity.

- What about intense religious activities like prayer, fasting, and Bible study? Does it help if we devote our lives to missionary work or social causes? Activities in which we express God's heart certainly have value. Spreading the message and experience of the kingdom of God benefits us too. But if spiritual maturity is all about performance goals, we might be better off spinning prayer wheels or chalking up sorties against social ills.

- Special powers to heal, deliver, lead people to the Lord, etc. are often taken as signs of spiritual maturity, but they are not sufficient.

Paul wrote that cultivating spiritual maturity in people is one responsibility of church leaders. God gives us leaders

> *for the equipping of the saints for the work of service, to the building up of the body of Christ; until we all attain to the unity of the faith, and of the knowledge of the Son of God, to a mature man, to the measure of the stature which belongs to the fullness of Christ. As a result, we are no longer to be children, tossed here and there by waves, and carried about by every wind of doctrine, by the trickery of men, by craftiness in deceitful scheming; but speaking the truth in love, we are to grow up in all aspects into Him who is the head, even Christ.* (Ephesians 4:12–15)

Paul pointed to Jesus as our model of spiritual maturity. Jesus never lived in a monastery; he worked as a building contractor in a rough country, during tough times. Jesus knew God thoroughly, but He knew men too. Jesus' relationship with God steered and energized His life in a hurting world. He knew the will of the Father and He obeyed it. Peter couldn't dissuade Jesus from it. Threats from religious authorities didn't deter Him from obedience. For Jesus, spiritual maturity meant applying every drop of His knowledge of God to His everyday life—no compromise, no inconsistencies, no holding back.

Jesus never trumpeted His maturity. An ambition to become mature in Christ doesn't seem like a bad thing, but as maturity develops, that ambition should give way to what someone called un-self-consciousness. That means taking our focus off ourselves and our spiritual growth. Instead, we fix our attention on

God and other people. We become a channel of God's love, truth, and power. We catalyze His work in the lives of others. Onlookers might discern and admire spiritual maturity in people, but the truly mature are likely to be unaware of it in themselves. They would blush and dismiss the suggestion.

So, You Want to Be Like Jesus?

(Context: John 11:1–46.)

What would you think if you received a call saying that a person's close friend was deathly ill, but the person did nothing for a day or two? You'd think they were callous, right?

Strangely, Jesus responded slowly when news came that Lazarus was ill. *"When therefore He heard that he was sick, He stayed then two days longer"* (John 11:6). By the time Jesus had walked from east of the Jordan river, up the wadis of the Judean desert, and across the mountain to Bethany, Lazarus had been dead four days (John 11:39). Is that uncaring or plain inhuman?

We find more odd behavior in the first part of the story. When Jesus announced His plan to travel to Bethany, the disciples were incredulous: "The Jews were just now seeking to stone You, and are You going there again?" (John 11:7–8).

The Jewish leaders' murderous intentions had grown as Jesus repeatedly offended them by healing people on the Sabbath.[1] He also claimed to be God's Son, equal to God—blatant blasphemy in their eyes.[2] But there's an unfortunately common reaction to good people; compared to them, ordinary folk can feel ashamed, and bad folk feel worse. An evil world hated Jesus because they felt His goodness highlighted their evil (John 3:20; 7:7).

---

1. Mark 3:1–6; Luke 13:10–17; 14:1–6; John 5:1–16.

2. Luke 5:21; John 5:17–18; 8:58–59; 10:30–39.

How can we become like Jesus when He acts like this or has this effect? Do we even want to be like Him? It's easy to build a religion of biblical bricks; living the transformed and empowered life that Jesus modelled for us to imitate is much harder. In His belated journey to Bethany, and in many other situations, Jesus violates our most respected values or flies in the face of common sense. But wait! Before we draw a line in the sand, stomp a foot, and say, "I will not go that far," why not give Jesus the benefit of the doubt? Let's accept that He is the Son of God (as Scripture tells us) and that He came to show us how to live as God's children—a life more abundant than we could ever attain naturally.

Jesus needed laser-like focus to live the way He did. He had to dismiss many presuppositions, values, and customs of society. He had to ignore the opinions and criticisms of those around Him, even when they said He was crazy or possessed by Beelzebub (Mark 3:20–30). He suppressed the human instinct for self-preservation. He led His followers into dangers they dreaded. Because of Him, His beloved friends mourned hopelessly when Lazarus died. Jesus' focus was elsewhere.

Life is different when you're the Son of an invincible King. For sure, Jesus was fully human, but although He understood and joined in human nature and culture, He refused to give human ideas and practices first place. His actions and words always rested on kingdom foundations—it's the logical way to live when you know the King. That's how He knew Lazarus' sickness would not end in death but in glory (John 11:4, 40). Walking in the daylight of His Father's will was safe, even in enemy territory (John 11:9–10).

So, how do we become like Jesus? He said it best: "Blessed are the poor in spirit, for theirs is the kingdom of heaven" (Matt. 5:3). Someone who is utterly poor has no possessions or resources. The poor are entirely empty and dependent on others. Similarly, the poor in spirit have nothing within themselves on which to draw; a gaping hole waits to be filled.

To the extent that we are free from the accumulated and treasured junk of human ways, we have inner room for the kingdom life. It does not mean isolating ourselves from others, disrespecting them, or disregarding the cultures in which we live. We can still have healthy fun at the poolside barbecue. But as the roots of our human ways are weeded from our spirits, we learn a new way of living—as children of the King. That's when our words start to bear fruit, and miracles increase to the glory of God—like they did for Jesus.

JOY TO THE WORLD

(Context: 2 Cor. 8:1–15.)

An unusual hiking trip began in 2011. It was unusual for two reasons: first, it took place in the Himalayan nation of Bhutan; second, the young king of Bhutan was the hiker. Bhutan had shrugged off the modern world's obsession with economic indicators and introduced a new measure—the Gross National Happiness Index. It's no surprise that it caught the media's attention; everyone wants to be happy. The king's aim was to connect with his subjects by visiting every rural household in the country. He cared so much about easing their hardships that he took the time to understand everyday life by trekking to their homes. King Five, as he had become known, inspired his people as an authority figure with compassion. He provided a lesson for us about the incarnation of Jesus, the supreme authority who shared our life in order to deal with our spiritual plight.

Trekking in the mountains of Bhutan is tough; trading heavenly splendor for a smelly stable is an inconceivable sacrifice. Jesus had no special door pass into life that enabled Him to enter as a grown man. He arrived as a baby and went through all the normal phases: teething, toddling, and teens. Jesus the carpenter probably dealt with awkward customers and even slipped with a hammer. Those experiences were part of the ordinary life of Jesus. They enabled Him to identify with the human condition, just as miles of mountain trails helped King Five to understand his subjects. In His incarnation, Jesus visited His people to do more than listen to needs (He already knew their needs); the King of kings stepped in to take action. As the perfect Son of God, Jesus freed us from the power of sin and death. King Jesus offers more than happiness; He brings deep and lasting joy to the world.

> *You know the grace of our Lord Jesus Christ, that though He was rich, yet for your sake He became poor, that you through His poverty might become rich.* (2 Corinthians 8:9)

Paul wrote those words to urge the church to continue the gracious work of giving to the needy. However, the lesson is more significant than that. We should model our entire lives and ministries on the incarnation of Jesus. There is immense spiritual power in sacrificing ourselves to serve others. Religious celebrities on raised stages certainly have their place, but a different kind of anointing comes with incarnational ministry. When we visit people in their homes, hear their hearts, and care for their needs, we can connect them with all the resources from the throne of God.

God Goes to Synagogue

(Parallels: Mark 3:1–6; Luke 6:6–11.)

[Jesus] went into their synagogue. And behold, there was a man with a withered hand. And they questioned Him saying, "Is it lawful to heal on the Sabbath?"—in order that they might accuse Him. And He said to them, "What man shall there be among you, who shall have one sheep, and if it falls into a pit on the Sabbath, will he not take hold of it and lift it out? Of how much more value then is a man than a sheep! So then, it is lawful to do good on the Sabbath." Then He said to the man, "Stretch out your hand!" And he stretched it out, and it was restored to normal, like the other. (Matthew 12:9–13. See too Luke 13:10–14.)

Some people might wonder why Jesus ever attended synagogue. After all, the reception was mixed. Of all the events of Jesus' life that happened in synagogues or the temple, 75 percent mention a negative reaction or conflict.[1] He was ejected from His childhood synagogue because the members doubted that God changes people—Jesus was no longer simply the carpenter's kid (Matt. 13:54–58; Luke 4:15–30). Traditions based on misunderstandings of God's heart contaminated Judaism. Synagogues included hypocrites and glory seekers reveling in a system

---

1. These figures come from my survey of 190 "events" recorded in the Gospels. Of events in a synagogue, 34 percent involved conflict; in the temple, 78 percent did.

that rewarded special people with special seats (Matt. 6:2, 5; 23:6). Yet Jesus attended (Matt. 4:23; 9:35; Luke 4:44; John 18:20). Why?

Jesus did not fit neatly into Jewish religion. He didn't come to endorse it but to fulfill God's plan revealed in Scripture. There was a difference, and often the sparks flew. He warned His followers to expect the same mixed reception (Matt. 10:17; 23:34; Luke 12:11; John 9:22; 12:42; 16:2).

Fast forward to the establishment of churches; similar contamination creeps into them too. Jesus' relationship with synagogues can teach us about our involvement in a church.

- Perhaps the best-sounding reason we give for church meetings is being in the presence of God. Certainly that happens. However, Jesus was always in His Father's presence; for that, synagogue was unnecessary. In fact, when Jesus needed spiritual replenishment, He withdrew to solitary places (Matt. 14:13, 23).

- Jesus attended because the Jewish culture, centered on synagogues and the temple, was primed to receive God in human form. Jews knew the Scriptures. They awaited the Messiah. A traveling rabbi had a ready platform. A synagogue was a great place to meet people who were somehow open to God. Our churches are too. Jesus didn't politely conform to traditions—He announced fulfilled promises of the kingdom. Open people rejoiced; it outraged devotees of the religious system. But they all heard the news.

- For Jesus, synagogues provided another opportunity to participate in God's work. Hungry and needy people went to synagogue. Jesus met some there—but only some. A mere 19 percent of His recorded ministry occurred in synagogues or the temple. Most of it (81 percent) happened in ordinary settings—in houses, on journeys, in streets, on mountains, and by a lake or river. I suspect that pattern allows for only a hesitant "thumbs up" to our special meetings held to minister to needs, receive teaching, or do evangelism. It's better that we should be salt and light, mostly "out there" in the world.

- That leaves one important activity. "Synagogue" means "bringing together." It was the place of communal prayer for God's people. Prayer meant more than petitions. It centered on Scripture reading as an act of worship focused on who God is and what He does. That led to petition and practical application. Jesus probably reveled in the ceremony on that level, especially knowing that He was fulfilling the prophecies and purposes of God. Even a dull church, if it's saturated in biblical theology, can be a healthy place to meet with and serve God. Spiritual health declines when people gather *mostly* to earn social respectability points, soothe feelings, air opinions, or indulge in relationships with each other rather than to welcome and respond to God's presence. Fundamentally, church is revamped synagogue—Jesus-followers gathering to praise Him, listen to Him, and make disciples who then disperse to obey Him.

Scripture tells us to gather with other disciples (Heb. 10:25). So, how should we approach those gatherings that we typically call "church"? We find no sign that Jesus or Paul ever tried to change the organization or practice of synagogue. Instead, they sought opportunities within the synagogues first—with open individuals, ordinary people, and leaders. We can look for those opportunities too. Speak the truth, minister in kingdom power in a gentle and loving way, accept rejection gracefully, and move on if necessary.

THE GRAND THEMES OF JESUS

Spectacular dances performed at epic events, like opening ceremonies for the Olympic Games, have grand themes. Choreographers weave the steps, music, costumes, backdrop, lighting, and props to maximum effect. Audiences gasp and cheer when they see everything syncing perfectly and the themes popping.

Jesus' life was a dance. Centuries of prophetic announcements formed the backdrop. The human spectrum surrounding Him became the props, with their aches and anxieties, doubts and demons, wickedness and weaknesses, pettiness and prejudices, fears and failures, hype, hypocrisy, and occasional humility. The grand themes? Well, if you had to summarize what Jesus accomplished on earth, what would you say?

- Many people immediately respond that He died to redeem us from sin to restore our relationship with God. That's true, of course. But let's not forget four other broad accomplishments or themes to His dance.

- The prophets outlined a little of God's father-nature; Jesus colored in their pencil sketch (John 14:8–9). Fathers are only really known as fathers by how they and their children interact. Only Jesus, the Son of God, could reveal a heavenly Father with a heartbeat.

- From Jesus' first proclamation to His last instructions, and through many demonstrations and explanations, He was all about the kingdom of God (Mark 1:15; Acts 1:3).

- He was faithful to make disciples who continued His work and made more disciples (John 17:6–19).

- John the Baptist said Jesus would send the Holy Spirit (John 1:33). Jesus returned to the Father to do just that, so His followers would have direction and power (John 16:7; 20:22; Acts 1:8).

Why is understanding all the grand themes in Jesus' dance important? Because Jesus called us to follow Him and become like Him. His dance is our dance . . . in part. He has completed the first and last items. No one has to repeat Jesus' sacrifice, and God has already poured out the Spirit. However, we should share about Jesus, explain what He did for us, be public in our interactions with the Father, extend His kingdom, and make more disciple-making disciples who live guided and empowered by His Spirit.

God continues to dance the last four of His themes. When we learn the steps of those themes, we will be in sync with God. Then we can expect the greatest blessing and fruit in what we do. Anything else might be a waste of time. So, do the grand themes pop when we examine our lives?

To close, a caution about learning. Many of us get caught up in classes and study, but learning is a slow process.[1] And we will never learn more than a fraction of God's ways. However, our relationship with the Father begins at the instant of adoption. A child that dances cares little about skill or understanding; its joy is in dancing with its father. Although we will never know exactly what God is doing, being with Him as He does it is enough. Following His lead is where the fun and fruit of dancing with God lie.

---

1. Someone said it takes 10,000 hours to become an expert in anything. That's five years of forty-hour weeks—enough to gain a bachelor's and a master's degree.

DANCING WITH GOD

(Context: John 5:1–21.)

Let's face it, God does the bulk of the positive and spiritually significant work in the world; our parts are minuscule. Yet He involves us. Why is that?

We can liken the relationship to a dance for couples—a dance consisting of set steps arranged in different sequences as the lead dancer chooses. We are like the partner following God's lead. For a couple to dance well, the follower needs to know the steps, not to lead but to follow gracefully. That includes responding to the leader's spontaneous moves. Dancing with God is about learning the steps so we're ready to follow His subtle cues.

Jesus spoke of God's dance when He said, *"The Son can do nothing of Himself, unless it is something He sees the Father doing; for whatever the Father does, these things the Son also does in like manner"* (John 5:19). Jesus never indicated that He sought feelings of God's presence; however, He watched for signs of God in action, and He knew how to respond. Living like Jesus means learning to dance with God the way Jesus did.

So, what are the dance steps and cues of God in the Gospels and Acts? Thirteen serve as steps, cues, or both, so this will be a longer piece. I suggest you take extra time, perhaps several days, to reflect on them and make them central to your dance with God.

1. Something happens that only God can do, often with significant timing. For example, the Spirit conceiving and anointing Jesus and coming at Pentecost, or angels opening prison doors.[1]

2. God announces or explains events by angels, visions, dreams, etc.[2] Stephen's summary of Israel's history shows how much God used such things to direct important events (Acts 7:1–38).

3. Signs point to things that God is doing.[3]

4. A person's faith is a cue that God can or will work.[4]

5. Needs (including sickness caused by sin or demonic involvement) and other opportunities to demonstrate miraculous power and God's glory are also cues (John 9:1–3; 11:4). The news about Jesus spread because He took care of needs. Jesus never performed signs to prove Himself to the cynical. Signs always pointed to the greatness and goodness of God.[5] Needs also led to the mobilizing of the disciples to meet those needs (Matt. 9:36–10:8). Faith and needs are combined with compassion in Matthew 20:29–34 (see too Mark 10:46–52).

6. Dislocation. God can use rejection when it forces a person to find a new community centered on following Jesus. For instance, the blind man who was kicked out of the synagogue (John 9:34–38). Rejection could explain why sinners, tax collectors, and Gentiles enter the kingdom more

---

1. Matt. 1:18; Luke 1:13, 35; John 1:32; Acts 2:1–4; 9:3–9; 10:17; 10:44; 16:14.

2. Matt. 1:20–21; 2:12–13, 19–23; Luke 1:11, 26–38; 2:8–14, 26–35; John 1:6–8, 32–34; Acts 5:19–20; 8:26–30; 9:10–18; 10:3–6, 11–16, 19–20; 13:2; 16:6–10; 18:9–10; 21:11; 22:17–21; 23:11; 27:23–26.

3. Matt. 2:2; 3:16–17; Mark 1:9–11; Luke 3:21–22; 7:19–23; Acts 2:5–12, 43; 8:5–7.

4. Matt. 8:10–13; 9:18, 22, 28–29; 15:28; 21:21–22; Mark 5:30–34; Luke 7:2–10; Acts 3:16; 14:9–10.

5. Matt. 8:27; 9:8; 14:14–21; Luke 5:12–15; Acts 3:1–3; 28:8–9.

easily than the religious (Matt. 21:31–32; Luke 5:30–32). Similarly, God puts new wine in fresh skins (Matt. 9:16–17).

7. Revelation. It comes to babes, not to the wise and intelligent (Matt. 11:25–26; Luke 24:31–32, 35). The Father uses it to draw open people (John 6:44–45).

8. People who are ready to understand and to change. Maybe they are humble and repentant, or interested, like the Ethiopian eunuch and Cornelius.[6]

9. The revealed will and ways of God. Jesus responded to things that He saw, often because of specific Scriptures about God's will and ways.[7] Prophecies come true.[8]

10. The Spirit impels (Mark 1:12; Acts 16:6).

11. Demons manifest, perhaps in an attempt to intimidate people and stop God from working.[9]

12. A sense of His presence (Luke 24:32).

13. Seeds that have already been sown and watered (John 4:35–38).

Learn to recognize these dance steps and cues. And keep those dancing shoes on.

---

6. Matt. 13:1–23; Luke 7:44–50; 19:1–10; John 5:6; Acts 2:37; 8:34–36; 10:2–4.

7. Matt. 21:12–16, 33–46; 26:54–56; Mark 14:49; Luke 24:25–27, 44–47.

8. Matt. 1:22–23; 2:4–6, 23; 3:1–3; 4:13–16; 8:17; 11:3–5, 10; 26:54–56; Mark 1:2–4; Luke 4:16–21; 18:31–33; Acts 4:25–28.

9. Matt. 8:28–34; Mark 1:21–26, 34; Luke 4:33–36, 41; Acts 13:6–12; 16:16–18.

Dance Partners

(Context: Acts 8:26–39; 10:1–11:18.)

Watching God's dance partners is the best way to learn about dancing with God. I hope we all have individuals around us who live as Jesus lived, observing what God is doing and responding with their small parts. For now, let's watch Philip and Peter in the book of Acts.

Both men were already on the dance floor with God. Philip, known as a Spirit-filled servant, had taken good news to Samaria (Acts 8:5–25). He had his gospel dance shoes on (Eph. 6:15). Peter, of course, was dancing too. To become dancers, we must begin dancing and improve as we go. Don't wait to master everything.

In Acts 8:26, an angel sent Philip to the Gaza road—a cue from God. Philip did whatever it took to get there. A carriage rumbled up, leaving a trail of dust. The Spirit prompted him to approach the carriage. He could hear the occupant reading Isaiah 53. The interest of the eunuch in such a key prophecy signaled that God was choreographing something. That's when we must know our part, our dance steps—and respond in time. Philip began with a simple question, *"Do you understand what you are reading?"* (Acts 8:30). It opened the door for Philip to ride with the eunuch and explain how Jesus fulfilled the passage in Isaiah. The eunuch's request for baptism was a further sign of his willingness to obey Jesus.

Acts 10 tells a more involved story. Cornelius and Peter each experienced God's coordinated leading. The centurion was open to God: he was devout, feared God, gave alms, and prayed continually. Perhaps seeds sown through living that way were sprouting. His cue came from an angel too, in a vision: accurate directions to Simon Peter, forty miles away in Joppa. As Cornelius' servants arrived in Joppa, hungry, sleepy Peter saw a vision that overturned his established thinking about cleanliness. Right then, the Spirit announced that three men were at the gate. The vision and the timed announcement cued Peter that God was dancing and he should join in. Peter danced his steps: a trip to Caesarea and a short message about Jesus. Like so many of the moves God makes in response to our parts, Peter did not expect the next one. The Holy Spirit fell on the Gentile listeners, so Peter baptized them.[1]

Both examples end with baptism, which indicates a person's willingness to make Jesus Lord and obey Him. Peter hung around for a few days. Presumably, he took the opportunity to teach more about Jesus and how to be His disciples. Dancing with God results in lives drawn to follow Jesus, and His kingdom extended—two of the grand themes of God.

These examples include just a few of the steps and cues still visible in Jesus' work today. We should familiarize ourselves and become proficient in all the possibilities, ready to dance our parts.

Jesus frequently did miracles to signal God's power and His care for the needy. That opened hearts to His teaching. But notice the twist in the disciples' case—God confirmed their message with signs that *followed* (Mark 16:20). Could that be how the next cycle begins—signs as a cue to new dancers? Imagine! God's dance becomes a Conga, sweeping the dance floor, swirling to Ethiopia and the ends of the Gentile earth as more and more disciples join in.

---

1. God had announced His plan to send the Spirit on Gentiles centuries earlier (Joel 2:28–32).

SOLITUDE OBSERVED

The news hit like a gut punch. He'd known John, His passionate and eccentric cousin, all His life. Now, evil forces, given free rein to rampage through King Herod's family, had swung an executioner's sword and struck off John's head. Was this a preliminary rumble of the thundering injustice and agony that Jesus would eventually face? Did John's fate cause Jesus to grapple with the prospect of His own death at the hands of hostile authorities? We'd understand if Jesus had shuddered and recoiled. Like us, perhaps He needed to catch His breath, get perspective, and refocus.[1] That required space, so He withdrew—at least, He tried to.

It's hard for a crowd to follow a boat, but not impossible to outrun one along the shoreline. So, when Jesus went ashore, the multitude was there. We resent interruptions, especially when we are emotionally drained and ready to relax; Jesus' compassion flowed as usual. He taught them, healed them, and then looked to heaven, blessed a few loaves and fish, and relieved their hunger (Luke 9:16). Finally, Jesus dismissed everyone and climbed a mountain to spend a few hours in prayer.[2]

What follows those hours is significant. Not only did Jesus have time to process John's death, He returned to do some of His most notable miracles. The disciples, vainly battling a wind that was carrying them off course by several miles,

---

1. Something similar happened in Gethsemane (Matt. 26:36–46).

2. John 6:14–15 gives another reason for Jesus' withdrawal. The Jews had recognized Jesus as the long-awaited messianic Prophet, and by implication, the king. Jesus knew their expectations of the Messiah were haywire, so He left.

saw Him like a phantom walking across the lake. Then, when Jesus got into the boat, the wind stopped (Matt. 14:32). Back on land, sick people only had to touch the fringe of His cloak to be cured, so great was His power (Matt. 14:35–36).

Luke, who claims to write in consecutive order (Luke 1:3), skips the lake scene. In his Gospel, Jesus' solitary prayer time led Him to ask the question of the ages, "Who do you say that I am?" (Luke 9:18–20). Perhaps His conversation with God about John had crystalized His thoughts. For the first time, He shared about His future suffering and the cost of discipleship (Luke 9:22–27).

Eight days later, Peter, James, and John hiked up a mountain with Jesus and, in exertion-induced drowsiness, watched. "*While He was praying*, the appearance of His face became different," and His clothing fluoresced with His unveiled glory.[3] Elijah and Moses appeared and talked with Jesus. The three followers were at a loss for words (Luke 9:28–36; 2 Pet. 1:16–18).

Overall, the disciples were so impressed with the results of Jesus' prayer times that they asked for a lesson (Luke 11:1).

The disciples have a key role in our study of Jesus' prayer life because they observed His solitude. No one spied on His prayer times; He must have recounted His words to the disciples, who often waited nearby anyway (Luke 22:31–32). They saw that, because Jesus shared human limitations, He depended on the direction and power of God. They saw prayer release them—with spectacular results.

With all their eyewitness accounts, the Gospel writers used only one Greek umbrella word (*proseuchomai*) for Jesus' prayer. It covered a range of things. Sometimes He sought guidance (Mark 1:35; Luke 6:12). At other times, He interceded for people (Luke 22:32; John 17:9–26). In grief, Jesus gained comfort and perspective. Gethsemane was an inner wrestling match to remain focused on

---

3. The Holy Spirit descended on Jesus as He prayed after His baptism (Luke 3:21).

God's will. Surrender saturated that prayer. Afterwards, He never faltered on His way to the cross. It seems that Jesus held different styles of conversations with God, just as we do with other people. No technical terms for types of prayer are necessary when they all amount to conversation.

He needed few words to present His needs; He was convinced that the Father knew already and gladly met them (Matt. 7:11). To get direction, insight, and wisdom, Jesus must have done a lot of listening, which requires silencing the inner chatter. Perhaps His "prayer" wasn't even verbal. Basking in the presence of God (what some call "communing with God") produces deep change as we come into union with Him.

We find no account of any special prayer times apart from synagogue meetings. He had a night session before choosing His disciples and was up early one morning before expanding His teaching sphere beyond Capernaum (Mark 1:35; Luke 4:42–43; 6:12). We have no record of Jesus praying formally, even though liturgical prayer was common in Judaism.[4] No one mentions team huddles in the back room behind the stage before ministry. (However, the silence doesn't mean those practices are wrong.) The clearest pattern is that Jesus eliminated distractions to be with the Father. His submissive conversations led to amazing incidents.

Jesus' retreats into solitude almost always included prayer. Perhaps we withdraw to avoid pressure and pain or to soothe ourselves with musical comforts or chocolate ice cream. If my goal is for God to influence my little world in my way, then I might slip away to lobby God, but I will be carrying my concerns about that world with me. If our prayers aim to check off a wish list of petitions as though we're stuffing an online shopping cart with goodies, checking out, and hoping for overnight delivery, then we take our list with us. But what if we withdraw from the list, too?

Jesus had goals but no obvious list. His times alone were never self-indulgent, aloof, or conceited. That's plain because He returned from those times to selfless service. He accepted interruptions where we might deflect them, especially when

---

4. The Lord's Prayer may derive from a liturgical prayer of the time.

we are emotionally drained. If we develop a prayer life like Jesus', God's power and love will flow through us even when circumstances rob us of any natural desire to serve and care. We're not the source of compassion and anointing, we are gatekeepers who decide how much they will flow.

LITTLE ANOINTED ONES

Each of our relational circles has its own labels for people who are popular, display admired characteristics, and who others want to imitate. What is admirable depends on the group and changes like every other trend; the language tags follow. I'm thinking of words like nice, sweet, cool, respectable, smart, hip, accomplished; you probably know others.

What words do we want spoken about us as Jesus-followers? Sometimes people say that I am kind, gentle, and safe. I like that. It gives me a warm feeling to think that I am accepted and respected for something. But after a while, the glow fades. Isn't there more to life than popularity tags?

Paul used a play on words that points us higher—to the core of what a Jesus-follower should desire as a reputation:

> *Now He who establishes us with you in Christ [the Anointed One (Christos)] and anointed (chrisas) us is God, who also sealed us and gave us the Spirit in our hearts as a pledge [or downpayment]. (2 Corinthians 1:21–22)*

We rarely hear it explained, but the word "Christian" is entwined with Jesus' honorary title, "Christ." *Christos* is the Greek equivalent of the Hebrew *mashiakh*. Both mean "anointed" and derive from the time when kings were installed by having oil poured on their heads until it ran down. Both words came into English hardly changed—Jesus Christ is Jesus the Messiah. The Messiah is

God's Anointed One (Ps. 2:1–2). So, the word "Christian" basically means "little anointed one."

Jesus began His ministry after being anointed with the Holy Spirit at His baptism (Matt. 3:16). The Spirit led and empowered Him (Matt. 4:1; Luke 4:14). One Sabbath, He read Isaiah 61:1–2 in the Nazareth synagogue: "The Spirit of the Lord is upon me, because He anointed me to preach the gospel . . ." (Luke 4:16–21). He followed His reading with a simple message—today it's fulfilled. Everything Jesus did—character and actions—supported His claim. Jesus' double nature means He is not just God in human form minus our fallen sinfulness, the Spirit of God saturates Him to overflowing.

Only one way leads to His kind of life—a second birth with water and the Spirit. When Jesus tried to explain that to Nicodemus, He referred to it as birth into the kingdom of God. It is marked by baptism—a public commitment to obey a new king—and a willingness to be blown through life by the Spirit, like a leaf in a breeze. The flesh stops running things; the will learns to allow the Spirit to lead and to rely on His power (John 1:12–13; 3:3–8). Jesus' kingdom life began with baptism in water and with the Spirit; ours does too (Matt. 3:11; John 1:33; Acts 1:4–5, 8; 2:1–4).

Jesus never gave complex explanations about the Spirit life, as Paul did; He kept things simple. Paul described various manifestations of the Spirit and brought perspective to them to counter disorder. Most of them are evident in Jesus' life, but He talked simply about being filled with *the Spirit* (John 14:16–17, 26; 20:21–22). The Spirit imparts life to us. He enlivens us for a purpose—to witness about the good news of Jesus and His kingdom. Whatever variety of teaching about the Holy Spirit we feel comfortable with, Jesus' simple words and ways should be our foundation.

To grow a reputation as little anointed ones, overflowing with God's Spirit, is a wonderful thing. That's what God has pledged to everyone who is established in Jesus, the Anointed One.

Brick Walls or Holograms?

(Context: John 14:1–14.)

Zane lay comatose in Intensive Care, hooked to monitors and drip lines. A dozen close family and friends had gathered in the adjacent room, gloomy, anxious, exhausted, but praying. The prognosis was ominous. Viral meningitis can cause brain damage and permanent disability.

Ed and I took our turn to pray at Zane's bedside. Careful not to dislodge a cord or tube, we laid hands on available parts of his arms and dutifully mumbled things to God. Immediately, Zane opened his eyes, blinked, and said, "Hey, guys. How you doing?" It was the most dramatic healing miracle I had ever witnessed.

I've been healed of a few minor ailments myself. Once, while traveling in Kenya, I climbed a hill with a thirty-pound backpack and set it down to enjoy the view. As I swung the pack up onto my shoulders again, click, my lower back screamed. It was painful, but I managed to stagger to the road and hitch a ride to Nairobi. At that time, God was working in a weekly prayer gathering. A few days later, I attended. The speaker gave an invitation to receive prayer. I stepped forward. An ordinary Kenyan man placed his hand on my spine, prayed in Jesus' name, and immediately the pain left.

"Truly, truly, I say to you, he who believes in Me, the works that I do shall he do also; and greater works than these shall he do; because I go to the Father." (John 14:12)

Are Jesus' words true or not? Remember what I said in the introduction about how we set limits on our Christlikeness. This is one of those topics in which we meet those limits, partly because we question Jesus' words. Various "barriers" project into our paths like holograms—looking as real as brick walls but penetrable. Here's a chance to examine some of them.

A sense of disqualification is a big one. Many people think that special training, experience, or understanding are required for us to minister like Jesus. Basic courses are useful—Jesus trained His disciples—but don't look for qualifications when Jesus doesn't. According to the Gospels, faith and compassion ignited miracles—develop them. And don't assume your stock of faith is too small; only a mustard seed's worth is necessary. Remember, faith focuses on God, not us. Faith is trust in His healing heart and power, not our own.

Even the self-assessment of our Christlikeness might be a hindrance if we see the glass as less than half full. It's better to recognize and enjoy the processes He uses to fill the glass gradually. Celebrate growth.

That sense of "not enough ———" is one thing; feeling too sinful is another. Many people think what they have done or said disqualifies them. Unfortunately, some Christian circles tend to create a culture of shame. Satan loves this. It begins with an unquestionable truth—we are sinners. However, that is a departing point, not a destiny or identity. Cycles of general confessions followed by absolutions are overly humble; focusing on our sinfulness too much stifles us. Satan smiles as he tucks people into that suffocating blanket. The Spirit, however, convicts us of specific sins and helps us to change and grow.

John addressed sin. Pretending we are always sinless is a deception; confessing sin results in God's forgiveness and cleansing. John wrote his letter so that we *may not sin*, but *if* we do, we have an Advocate to deal with it (1 John 1:8–2:2). The good news is that we are freed from the power and shame of sin, freed to grow more like Jesus. On the occasions when we do sin again, we have every opportunity to get back on track. Sin certainly separates us from God, but it never has to be a lasting disqualification.

Perhaps the most common barriers that keep people from doing the works of Jesus are ignorance or unbelief. Either we have not been taught that Jesus told us to do signs and wonders, or we don't take His words at face value. Perhaps we don't want to! A fear of failure is understandable. No one wants to look foolish when nothing seems to happen after praying for a healing. No one wants to disappoint hurting people, either. But those fears are simply extensions of our distrust of Jesus' words and of focusing on ourselves.

To do Jesus' miraculous works, consider the following steps:

1. Believe what He said about us doing greater things than Him.

2. Be alert for opportunities and ask Him what He wants to do with them.

3. Be bold to speak healing over people unless He indicates otherwise.

4. Ask the person if they noticed any change.

5. If the change was partial, pray again for complete healing (Mark 8:22–26).

Don't get discouraged by minimal outcomes. By persevering, our faith grows, and we learn to focus more on Him and less on those projected barriers.

Jump School— Miracle Maneuvers

(Context: Luke 5:1–11.)

We know little about the early days of Jesus' ministry. John provides insights into time that Jesus spent by the Jordan where He first met Simon Peter, and His days in Jerusalem. Luke tells us how the synagogue congregation in Nazareth violently rejected Jesus, and that He moved to Capernaum.

One day, Jesus visited Simon Peter's home after a synagogue meeting. Peter's mother-in-law had a fever, which Jesus rebuked. Later, Jesus borrowed Peter's boat from which to teach a crowd on the beach. Following the message, Jesus did a miracle that rearranged the fishermen's lives.

> *When He had finished speaking, He said to Simon, "Put out into the deep water and let down your nets for a catch." And Simon answered and said, "Master, we worked hard all night and caught nothing, but at Your bidding I will let down the nets." And when they had done this, they enclosed a great quantity of fish, and their nets began to break. (Luke 5:4–6)*

So great was the catch that Simon Peter's crew had to call for help. "Hey, James and John, bring your boat quickly, or we'll lose 'em." They were all amazed because that night there hadn't been any sign of fish. Peter was so struck by the miracle that he fell at Jesus' feet, convicted by comparison. "Depart from me, for I am a sinful man, O Lord!" (Luke 5:8). Life changed for Peter. He no longer referred to Jesus as Master but as Lord. It also launched Peter & Co. into a new kind of business—fishing for men. The partners left everything to follow Jesus.

How did Jesus have such an impact on men who, until then, might have been little more than His acquaintances? It's not that Jesus had a clever new strategy for locating or netting fish; rather, it was His presence and His authoritative word that made the difference to Peter. "I will do as you *say*."[1]

Most people take their time to build new relationships. Trust has to be earned, and common interests discovered through conversations and shared experiences. Jesus is exceptional. He parachutes behind walls of customary reserve and privacy using three parachutes to invade lives: love, truth, and power. He lands deftly facing the real me, looking straight into the eyes of ignorance, independence, cynicism, self-protection, shame, pride, or whatever separates us from real life. His love caresses the scarred hearts of the rejected or un-affirmed. His truth illuminates shadowy strongholds built of little white lies. His miraculous power wows and rattles minds, urging them to listen to the Spirit. Jesus' arrival transforms. Peter & Co. witnessed miracle power that day, and it jolted them away from business as usual onto a fast track to follow Him.

As Jesus' present-day disciples, we can take parachute lessons from Him. You see, when Jesus parachutes into our lives, He recruits and trains us to join Him on jumps and to see other lives begin to change, too, because of love, truth, and power. Jesus runs a jump school.

---

1. *Rhema* is the Greek word translated "bidding" or "say."

Jump School—Love Lessons

(Context: Luke 7:34–50.)

Often, our minds scan the scenes described in the Bible too quickly. If we are to grasp the details so the story comes alive, we need to slow down. Let's do that as Jesus met with a Pharisee for a meal in a setting that likely opened onto a courtyard.

Tables had stubby legs in those days. Diners lay on their sides on cushions and ate from a low platform. While Jesus and His host reclined, an immoral woman arrived. The gossip mill had told her that Jesus was there, so she took advantage of the semi-public setting. Ignoring the politely irritated Pharisee and his shocked servants, some of whom were sniggering, she approached Jesus.

> *Standing behind [Jesus] at His feet, weeping, she began to wet His feet with her tears, and kept wiping them with the hair of her head, and kissing His feet, and anointing them with the perfume. . . . He said to her, "Your sins have been forgiven." (Luke 7:38, 48)*

Notice the crescendo. As she stood over Jesus, weeping, her tears fell and splashed on His feet. Feeling embarrassed but receiving no rebuke, she knelt to dry His feet with what she had—her hair. Again, no negative reaction. She began to kiss His feet. Then she opened a vial she carried and began lavishing perfume on them, relishing His acceptance, ignoring other people's reactions.

Jesus addressed the Pharisee first. A brief interactive parable made it clear that the woman's expression of love was proportional to how much she had been forgiven. But Jesus had said nothing to her so far, so how did she know His forgiveness?

It probably began with Jesus' reputation as a friend of sinners (Luke 7:34). Perhaps fellow outcasts had shared how He accepted them not *for* what they were but *as* they were. He had offered them a new life, dignity in place of shame. Her sinful life had become so unbearable that she sought out Jesus. Finding Him, and experiencing His calm approachability, her wretchedness and expectant longing for relief finally overflowed in tears. Like the Pharisee, most people bristled when they saw her, mumbling judgment on her and Jesus. Minding their own business, they avoided guilt by association. However, at each stage of her expression of love, Jesus simply accepted her, probably with a gentle, caring smile.

The woman was bold because she anticipated forgiveness based on His reputation of love. He acknowledged her expectation: "Your faith has saved you; go in peace" (Luke 7:50).

Exercising Jesus' kind of acceptance is akin to defusing bombs. Sliding probing comments or actions into blemished lives can trigger explosions of denial, minimization, defensiveness, and rejection. That's why few of us dare to develop love beyond tinkering. But there was something disarming about Jesus' approach. When He pointed to an issue, He did not condemn. His observations were undeniably true, yet He provided a clear path to freedom and health. When people know that someone wants the best for them and has solutions, they are more likely to allow probing that heals. Accepting people as they are is entry-level love; it provides an opening for greater touches of God's love. God's love seeks the highest for a person, and that highest is found in a transforming relationship with Him.

As we surrender more to God, we become more like Jesus. When we are saturated in the Father's love for us, His love rises within and overflows to others—even social misfits—regardless of what they give back. (His wisdom, truth, and power bubble out too.) It no longer matters what others think of us; we will think God's thoughts toward them.

Acceptance is just one of many expressions of love; service and its unattractive cousin, sacrifice, are important too. Jesus used them all like parachutes to float across walls to free people imprisoned by social rejection, disease, and sin. To love like Jesus, we must soar over barriers as He did: serve and sacrifice; hear people's stories without flinching; be genuine in our desire for their best in relationship with God; and provide a helping hand as they take steps toward the new life.

Jump School— Truth 'Chutes

(Context: John 4:5–42.)

Remember those late summer barbecue feasts in the garden when you sat down to enjoy a juicy burger, and then the yellowjackets swooped in? They flew over your shoulder, buzzing past your ear as if to taunt you. Then they para-glided to your plate, circled, and landed with their undoubtedly filthy feet right on your next bite. Arms flailed, kids shrieked, and someone upset their meal on the grass. To some people with dark secrets, Jesus can seem like a pesky wasp when it comes to truth and its companion, wisdom.

A woman was mildly irritated when she found Jesus hovering by her water source near Sychar. She tried to wave Him off by questioning why a Jewish man would ask a Samaritan woman for a drink (John 4:9). He persisted with an offer of living water. She swiped back, doubting what He said and jabbing at His authority, "You are not greater than our father Jacob, are You?" (John 4:12). Jesus circled and offered again, "a well of water springing up to eternal life" (John 4:14).

This time, she did the equivalent of what I do to solve the wasp problem—give them a morsel. Perhaps she hoped that showing interest in His "water" would humor Him. Maybe He would snatch the scrap and fly away, as most wasps do. But this one was focused on something bigger. He landed on the intimate truth that she was in a relationship with a man who was not her husband. This "wasp" had parachuted right behind her privacy hedge—not stinging, but sharp, nonetheless.

In response, many people would reach for the swatter or the pesticide. However, she took a bold step and allowed Jesus to settle on her plate of touchy truth. "Sir, I perceive that You are a prophet" (John 4:19). She nudged Him as though attempting to steer Him to the edge of the plate with a fork. "What's your opinion about places of worship?" Jesus cleverly maneuvered around her deflection and drew her to more truth: things are changing, salvation and a new depth of worship are coming. Again, she allowed Him to flutter closer. *"I know that Messiah is coming"* (John 4:25). That's when Jesus dropped the final truth bomb, *"I who speak to you am He"* (John 4:26).

This brave Samaritan had accepted uncomfortable truths about herself and the inaccuracies and inadequacies of Jewish and Samaritan religion. These, and Jesus' final comment, had such an impact that she left her waterpot and returned to the city with a pounding question, "This is not the Messiah, is it?" (John 4:28–29). Truth spread around Sychar. People came out to see Jesus. Many believed and received further teaching, just as all disciples do when they respond positively to Him (John 4:30, 39–42).

Remember this about parachutists, though—they have the shortest life expectancies of any deployed troops. Those armed with truth and wisdom meet the fiercest resistance; love and miracle power are less likely to be repelled.

Remember the spring feast called Passover, late in Jesus' ministry? Jesus had cracked a whip in the outer courts, upset tables, and set people shrieking. Religious leaders responded like pest exterminators, "seeking how to destroy Him" (Mark 11:18). They feared the "wasp-friendly" multitude, so they worked stealthily. First, they swiped at Jesus' authority, but He was too agile (Mark 11:27–33). He circled back with a pointed parable about tenant farmers who mismanaged a vineyard. Offended by the truth, and rejecting wisdom, the leaders tried to seize Him (Mark 12:1–12). They set various traps and sprayed questions at Him, but Jesus was too clever by far (Mark 12:13–34).

Clearly, Jesus was never afraid to speak truth to anyone. True, He sometimes packaged it in parables to see who would unwrap it and who would just admire the wrappings. We often avoid saying anything tough. If necessary, we prefer to offer tidbits to see what the response is. We politely deliver truth in a soft sandwich of flattering niceties hoping it will slide down smoothly. Jesus presented truth simply but without being rude, angry, or insulting. He knew what would happen that Passover; He'd heard about the death warrant.

Engaging in conflict verges on the suicidal. Paratroopers jump into hostile territory only after carefully calculating the stakes. Jesus was no fool; He knew there would be gains in Sychar and a costly setback in Jerusalem. Eventually, the religious leaders did succeed in trapping Jesus—in a garden. They contained Him and exterminated Him.

Now, we know the end of the story—Jesus rose again. But don't forget those religious leaders. You see, allowing truth or wisdom to settle and coming to terms with them are always optional. It's the same with love and power. Some people, like the Samaritans, will change; others will brush them off, perhaps squish them, preferring the status quo of shadow-land. Regardless of the response, Jesus and His followers never stop hovering, dropping in wherever they can, nurturing those who respond positively.

Blessings: A Recipe

Could it be that "blessings" are what humans crave most? We relish the pleasure and encouragement of parents and others who are close to us; we avoid their displeasure and shrivel at discouragement. Beyond words, blessings come in the form of fame and fortune, offspring and opportunities, peace and perks—anything that boosts our happy-hormones. Blessings are often subjective.

One nameless woman in a crowd had a rather odd idea. She shouted to Jesus,

"Blessed is the womb that bore You, and the breasts at which You nursed." But He said, "On the contrary, blessed are those who hear the word of God, and observe it." (Luke 11:27–28)

Who knows why she focused on anatomy instead of simply referring to, "Your mother, Mary"? Anyhow, Jesus corrected her thinking. The honor of doing something for Jesus, being associated with Him, or receiving a unique position is little compared to the blessing of obedience. Now, some people will point out that Mary *was* blessed as she carried Jesus (Luke 1:42–48). True, but Mary bore Jesus only because she had bowed humbly to her assignment and believed what God said. Blessed lives are built on the rock-solid foundation of living how God says to live (Luke 6:47–49).

What does this have to do with being like Jesus? Well, Jesus lived in maximum obedience and, as a result, received the most famous name—a supreme blessing (Phil. 2:9–11). But let's also consider the way in which Jesus bestowed blessing—and how we offer it. To do so, we will think about a blessing that Jesus extended to John the Baptist.

John the Baptist wanted clarity. Was Jesus the Expected One (Messiah), or not? John sent two disciples to ask. They watched Jesus heal people and cast out evil spirits. Then Jesus told them to report back to John with a résumé that fulfilled important messianic prophecies—except the ones about bringing justice (Isa. 29:18–19; 35:4–6; 61:1–2). Jesus added an offer: "Blessed is he who keeps from stumbling over Me" (Luke 7:17–23).

John was about to be thrown into a desert dungeon to live at the whim of foxy King Herod, his wicked wife, and her dancing daughter. "Jesus was challenging John not to stumble while justice delayed. He would complete His messianic task in stages; freedom for some captives would have to wait."[1] Jesus didn't want John to trip in his conviction about who Jesus was; walking tall, even through persecution, would bless John. Perseverance was worth the price.

Now, if I am attached to someone, I want them to succeed in a way that blesses them but also satisfies and blesses me. That tempts me to pressure people. I want loved ones to give themselves to Jesus, so I might overdo the frequency and intensity of my persuasion. But Jesus didn't beg John to stand firm. Jesus didn't need John to succeed in faith to benefit Him. He cared deeply about blessing John, but none of His care had selfish motives.

As I offer advice, I want to preserve the relationship and maintain my friend's acceptance and support of me. So, it's risky challenging people to do things that come with a price tag of pain. Most people will suggest a little self-discipline to help someone lose a few pounds or win a swimming contest; few of us become Olympic coaches. Yet strong, clear, and firm instruction is Jesus' way, because

---

1. *The Name Quest – Explore the Names of God to Grow in Faith and Get to Know Him Better*, by John Avery, Morgan James Publishing, 2015. Page 261. Used with permission.

His goal for us is extra-ordinary. He wants us to be more than "nice" people; He desires us to become like Him.

If we are used to begging and persuading, or sugar-coating our words, Jesus' take-it-or-leave-it approach will seem cold and idealistic. Jesus simply and gently holds out blessing. He never fights that fundamental human attribute called free will. Aren't we more mature when we take Jesus at His simple word, "Continue to follow me and do what I say, and you will be blessed"? We shouldn't need our arms twisted; we shouldn't twist other people's arms.

JESUS' "FAILURES"

(Context: Matthew 19:16–30. Parallels: Mark 10:17–31; Luke 18:18–30.)

Jesus was no failure. But when we consider the outcome of some of Jesus' ministry encounters, I think you'll agree that we would not naturally rate them as successes. If we put ourselves into the scenes, most of us would chalk them up as failures.

Matthew 19:16–26 is the story of a man who allowed his human accomplishments to keep him from living the kingdom life. Matthew, Mark, and Luke provide us with a composite sketch of a rich young ruler who approached Jesus seeking directions to eternal life. He recited a list of religious achievements but knew something was missing. Jesus told him to sell everything, give the proceeds to the poor, and follow Him. The price was beyond him. The man parted from Jesus with a heavy heart.

> *When the young man heard [Jesus'] statement, he went away grieved; for he was one who owned much property. And Jesus said to His disciples, "Truly I say to you, it is hard for a rich man to enter the kingdom of heaven." (Matthew 19:22–23)*

If I shared truth with someone, and it turned out the way it did for Jesus, I would kick myself. "Why did I say *that* to him? If only I had been more sensitive. I should have given him an easier option. I could have encouraged him for his obedience to the other commandments. Oh no, perhaps I ruined him for eternity." If a quick decision to sign up for an easy club membership was the goal, we likely failed. Perhaps we wanted a happy and affirmed new friend; instead, we alienated someone. Of course, sometimes we do handle things badly, but the failures of others to accept an invitation are not always our own failures.

Jesus was probably sad as the man departed. But Jesus was not a failure. He gently pointed the way to eternal kingdom life; the young ruler chose to walk away. For him, the price was too high.

We never read of Jesus running. He never catches someone by the sleeve, pleading, "Hey, wait a minute. Let me explain." Jesus never scrambles to salvage a situation or score a point. Jesus always honors people's choice to decline His offer. But He leaves the door open, hoping for minds and hearts to change later.

The Cringe Factor

[Jesus'] mother and brothers came to Him, and they were unable to get to Him because of the crowd. And it was reported to Him, "Your mother and Your brothers are standing outside, wishing to see You." But He answered and said to them, "My mother and My brothers are these who hear the word of God and do it." (Luke 8:19–21)

Every account of this incident makes us cringe. We get the impression that Jesus kept His family waiting. That seems rude. Healthy humans give their best to their loved ones, don't they? Most of us would have asked the crowd to step aside so we could respond to our mother and brothers.

It's not the only time Jesus responded differently than us. He did not run after the rich young ruler to offer better terms of discipleship (Matt. 19:22). Jesus rebuked super-loyal Peter but let Judas slip out unconfronted (Matt. 16:22–23; John 13:21–30). He dodged admiring fan clubs who were ready to make Him king (John 6:15). Our culture craves trust and loves to give the appearance of trusting others. Jesus was realistic and honest; He did not entrust Himself to people because He knew human nature (John 2:24–25). Jesus related differently to everyone.

So, if our goal is to become more like Jesus, how do we deal with the cringe factor? We don't want to be uncaring about people, uninvolved, disrespectful, aloof, or detached—Jesus never was. Habitual isolation is unhealthy. Self-centeredness is a sin. If we think those attitudes and behaviors are the result, we prefer to avoid Jesus' style.

If we are honest, the way in which we relate to other people is not entirely selfless and healthy. We pattern our relationships around a mixture of motives: fears of being alone or rejected, a need for affirmation and acceptance, a longing for companionship, a compulsion to meet other people's needs, and a fear of straying from cultural norms. Those motives can reach another "meta" level: What will other people say about me if . . .? Will they accuse me of rejecting them or being unfriendly toward another person? Will they perceive me as unloving, selfish, aloof, etc.? Bottom line: we want to be known as someone who relates well within our circles (never mind the social misfits that many people dismiss); we think that, to be a good person, we must follow the relationship rules of the groups we are part of. Jesus was free of all those motives.

Having said that, Jesus was no social rebel. One characteristic that made Him different was the "group" He most identified with. The key to understanding how He ticked was His attention to doing the word of God. Jesus was so thoroughly submitted to God that God's rule colored every aspect of His own life—including relationships. Obedience is still His friendship factor (John 15:14). Those who hear and do God's will become closer to Jesus than those who do not—even natural family. The obedient are His group.

If that way of relating was true for Him, shouldn't it be true for us as well? How would our lives change if we were free from unhealthy motives and formed our friendships and spiritual family in the same way as Jesus, with those who do His will?

SECRET ARTS

(Context: Matthew 11:16–19. Parallel: Luke 7:31–35.)

One secret art of influencers like politicians and activists is telling people what to think. Such people happily alert us to the lost, the losers, the dirty, and the dangerous. First, they paint a picture of people or practices that they consider to be bad in various ways, perhaps even hostile. They smear everyone in a group or everything about a practice with the same dark stain. They add advice about how to protect one's interests or punish the evil. Finally, they prescribe remedies for the bad actors or actions.

By maintaining high truth content while doctoring the significance of each piece of evidence, truth is twisted to serve a purpose. A little fluorescent highlighting helps, but broad brush strokes are sufficient. Apply either over the course of several weeks and the picture forms easily. Imaginations and discussions with friends are quite capable of adding enough color and detail to bring it alive with relevance in people's minds. Passions become inflamed. Leaders rise up to rally eager crowds to the cause. The results make headlines and fill the history books.

Jesus would have none of that dark art. He treated everyone as an individual. He did not lump people together and assume that a majority were evil just because a minority deserved a reputation. And, of course, His criteria were God's values, not those derived from politics or popular causes. Even Jesus' religious opponents acknowledged that He was impartial, although it angered them (Mark 12:14). They lumped Him with the bad guys—a *friend of tax-gatherers and sinners!"* (Matt. 11:19). "Like arrows, the words were designed to hurt, but they unintentionally advertised the wide embrace of God."[1]

Children were no nuisance to Jesus—He received and blessed them. He gave women respect as friends and supporters. He never cringed or hesitated in His interactions with Gentiles. He gave despised tax collectors the same opportunities to turn and receive forgiveness as everyone else. One even became a disciple. His openness extended down the scale of supposed weirdness and wickedness to Samaritans and lepers. Jesus demonstrated a new depth of love that included everyone—even enemies, no matter who defined them.

What pictures are being painted by your persuasive friends and family, politicians, religious leaders, the media, or other influencers? Do you investigate their claims? Do you seek alternative sources of information? Have you ever tried getting to know the people targeted by the pointing fingers? Most important, we should ask God to give us His heart for everyone we meet and for every issue that arises.

Of course, sometimes there are elements of truth in the designations of evil and its actors. It's then that we need the greatest discernment to recognize the fuzzy edges of the truth and to respond with wisdom. Maturity requires us to discover God's heart and let it inform our thinking. To love people the way Jesus did, we must develop His art.

---

1. *The Name Quest – Explore the Names of God to Grow in Faith and Get to Know Him Better*, by John Avery, Morgan James Publishing, 2015. Page 253. Used with permission.

Intimate Encounters

Before you read this, do a little exercise. Think about the life and ministry of Jesus as we know it from the Gospels. Of course, He spent the most time with His family and His disciples. But beyond them, what were Jesus' most intimate encounters (based on the topic, time spent, and emotional depth)?

Finished? How does your list compare to my top ones?

- The promiscuous woman of Samaria (John 4).

- An adulteress (John 8:1–11).

- Mary Magdalene, clinging to Jesus when she met Him by His tomb (John 20:11–18).

- Mary and Martha in their grief at Lazarus' death (John 11).

- An evening with Nicodemus (John 3:1–21).

- Mary with the nard (John 12:1–8).

- Staying with Zaccheus (Luke 19:1–10).

- A woman with a hemorrhage (Matt. 9:20–22).

- Peter, James, and John at the transfiguration (Matt. 17:1–8).

Perhaps your list differs from mine, but I see an interesting pattern. Women head my list and, shocking as it seems, in two cases, the interactions included their sexual relationships. Typical Christian teaching says that, outside of marriage, men and women should keep their distance and avoid intimate conversations. Jesus seems to have missed that teaching. So how do we respond to the pattern?

One answer is to make Jesus the exception. I.e., Jesus is the perfect Son of God; He could do whatever He wanted. However, we are told that He was *tempted in all things as we are, yet without sin* (Hebrews 4:15). Did Jesus resist temptation because He was special? That misses the point of the verse: Jesus is like us but still overcame temptation. So perhaps the women that He encountered were not tempting. Somehow, I doubt that they went around with sacks over their heads.

Doesn't this pattern of intimate encounters make a statement about our new life as children of God? Jesus valued women and treated them honorably, not as dispensable playthings or possessions. He cared enough to listen to their hearts. He could speak into their pain, shame, and confusion. He accepted their affection. His longer-standing relationships with women like Mary Magdalene were probably consistent with Paul's counsel to Timothy to treat *the older women as mothers, and the younger women as sisters, in all purity* (1 Timothy 5:2).

Jesus demonstrated kingdom behavior—the life we are inheriting. He was an example of how to have an intimate friendship without straying into an inappropriate relationship. There are plenty of opportunities for today's men (and women) to do the same!

Fine Wine

Most of Jesus' miracles changed lives by meeting debilitating needs. Because of that, we tend to think needs are always a factor in the miracle equation. It sets many of us calculating the best formula to invoke divine help: emphasize the severity of the problem, appeal to God's power, remind Him of previous miracles, flex the faith muscles, and recruit a squad of persistent prayer warriors. That way of thinking contains some truth, but there's more to learn about miracles.

What about those times when Jesus acted with little or no sign of a human need? Remember how He walked on the lake and allowed Peter to join Him (Matt. 14:25–32). Neither act seems necessary. Surely, He and Peter could have crowd-sourced their tax bill when it came due. Instead, Jesus directed Peter to catch a fish, which had a coin in its mouth (Matt. 17:24–27). After rising from the dead, Jesus miraculously entered a locked room without even knocking (John 20:26). No needs were met, but in each case, the disciples saw His divinity. Peter learned about the power and provision available to him as a son of the kingdom.

It's no surprise that God never does shoddy work; it would be out of character. After seeing Jesus heal a deaf mute, onlookers *"were utterly astonished, saying, 'He has done all things well; He makes even the deaf to hear, and the dumb to speak'"* (Mark 7:37). Again, He could have left the blind man at Bethsaida with severe astigmatism; instead, He laid hands on him a second time and completed the healing (Mark 8:22–26).

What about that poor, innocent fig tree (Matt. 21:18–20)? Surely there was no need to curse and shrivel it. Yet even that strangest of Jesus' actions had a purpose. It provided a faith lesson but also starred in a final, damning prophetic drama performed on Israel's center stage: for the nation that had failed to bear the fruit God sought, the season had ended fruitless. Judgment loomed. But fig trees grow like weeds in Mediterranean climates; God would propagate more. The value of the message easily outweighed the cost to the tree.

Even some miracles that addressed needs were not entirely necessary. No one dies for lack of champagne at a wedding. Multitudes could fast a meal or two with few ill effects, though perhaps the frailer ones needed some nourishment.

Do we hesitate to ask God for help if the severity factor in our equation seems too small? Maybe we settle for partial answers because we are taught to be politely content. We live in a world of shortages; isn't it greedy to want basketfuls of leftovers from a satisfying meal (Matt. 14:20; 15:37)? And, like the headwaiter at the wedding in Cana, we have come to expect cheap boxed blends, rather than fine wine. Turning water into plonk would satisfy and even impress us. Jesus goes further; He manifests glory by lavishing the best on us when it's least expected (John 2:9–11).

Let's allow God to expand our ideas about miracles. He's a Father who gladly gives what is good to His children (Matt. 7:11). By watching the Wonder Worker, we learn of a God *who is able to do exceeding abundantly beyond all that we ask or think* (Eph. 3:20).

FRUIT INSPECTION

(Context: Matthew 7:15–20. Parallel: Luke 6:43–45.)

After his vacation on a tropical island, my English language student came to class with pictures of various fruits. So, part of our lesson involved him showing me his grainy photographs while I tried to identify the fruits. Having lived in Africa and the Caribbean, I recognized starfruit, cocoa, guava, jackfruit, and durian. The distinctive way that papayas hang under an umbrella of leaves at the top of a naked trunk gave them away. But others, like noni (even though I had seen it often), stumped me. Because noni is ugly and smells unpleasant, it's not widely eaten; rather, it's mostly used for skin products and food supplements.

There was nothing disagreeable about the fruit of Jesus' life. His words were true. His miracles brought glory to God. No matter how people treated Him, His responses were gracious. Selfishness and evil never erupted from His heart (Matt. 15:19–20).

Jesus paid attention to fruit in others too. He knew what He was looking for and how it developed. Life-fruit depends on the root—no exceptions. *"You will know them by their fruits,"* said Jesus (Matt. 7:16, 20; 12:33–37). And spiritual fruitfulness sprouts from faithfulness, which is rewarded with greater responsibility (Luke 16:10; 19:17). There are no shortcuts. Young tree fruit might enthusiastically start to form, crowding the twigs, bursting with vibrant promises of bounty, but that guarantees nothing. The would-be-followers who trotted up, excited but not actually ready to join Jesus, were like the tiny "June-drop" apples that litter orchards weeks before harvest. They fell away at His warnings about discomfort and His challenges to prioritize and focus on the kingdom of God

(Luke 9:57–62). Likewise, the boasts of wise and experienced people, standing tall as they volunteer at every opportunity, count for little. During Jesus' trial, Peter was so unripe that he denied knowing Jesus. For Jesus, fruit alone revealed the true condition of a person.

Although Jesus was realistic about human behavior, and never entrusted Himself to anyone, He did not despair of people (John 2:23–25). Knowing the roots and fruits of human nature turns some people sourly cynical and bitterly critical of others. It could leave us despairing that humankind is worthless and hopeless. Another response is to ignore our own failings and become proud and aloof. Jesus had none of those responses. He was impartial in His treatment of people (Matt. 22:16). He accepted that many who started well would fall away and that yields would vary. He gave people every reason to believe in Him but left them to decide how they would respond. He encouraged faith steps but allowed for retreats too. Jesus expects and demands nothing of us; He invites us to new life, provides power, and hopes we will accept. Our responses judge us (John 3:17–21).

Roots are the key to the fruit. Much of Jesus' teaching focused on changing people's roots: their wrong thinking, morality, and attachments. He tended His followers like promising young trees knowing that fruit may take years to develop. Given time, disciples can become like their Master, and do greater works (Matt. 10:25; John 14:12). Two things make the difference.

- Like Jesus, we need to be humble (Matt. 11:29). Humility includes being real about who we are—strengths and weaknesses. It's the starting point for turning from our wild roots to new life.

- Jesus pictured us as branches attached to the rootstock of the vine (John 15:1–11). By keeping His commandments, we abide in Him. That in turn, makes us fruitful. New life and fruit depend on that attachment, which begins when we start following Him in faith.

High Fives

Thirty-five pairs of followers gradually congregated at a pre-arranged rendezvous. Chattering excitedly in fours, sixes, and eights, they cut short each other's stories in a rush to tell their own. Every now and then, there'd be a cheer and palms would slap in high fives. They'd been skeptical about the harvest when they set out, feeling pretty timid, too. But things had happened just as their rabbi had said. "People of peace" had received them and their news. They'd been welcomed, fed, housed, and introduced to others. Sick people had recovered. Even demons had been subject to the followers in Jesus' name. It was true, the harvest *was* ready. Once all seventy had returned and compared notes, Jesus brought perspective to the whole exercise:

> *I was watching Satan fall from heaven like lightning. Behold, I have given you authority to tread upon serpents and scorpions, and over all the power of the enemy, and nothing shall injure you. Nevertheless, do not rejoice in this, that the spirits are subject to you, but rejoice that your names are recorded in heaven.* (Luke 10:18–20)

What did Jesus mean when He said Satan fell like lightning? Was He clapping and cheering a victory by the disciples? Was He humoring their excitement or quietly affirming their recapture of swaths of enemy territory? We will never know for sure, but His enthusiasm sounds muted until we realize the weight of His other words. They're easier to understand. "Rejoice that your names are written in heaven." The idea being that God's subjects are registered in the royal records, and remembered. Jesus' followers have spiritual authority when acting on His behalf, but inclusion in that indelible list is unbeatable.

With everything about Jesus, there would be something seriously wrong if we did not see evidence that He practiced what He taught. So it's no surprise that in all the miracle stories we find no record of Him celebrating. That doesn't mean He wasn't filled with pleasure or happy to help people, but nowhere does He make a big deal of anything He did. Unlike us, right? Jesus had fully functional emotions, but the fist-pumping, back-slapping, whooping ones are never mentioned. He wept while Lazarus lay entombed, but He did no cartwheels after He raised him—and no high fives.

Typically, we think that doing signs and wonders is a high bar requiring special training and spiritual prowess. That's contrary to Jesus' view. He considered it easy to perform miracles—just ask in faith. He liberally authorized His followers to do them and promised results. However, perhaps the most sobering comment that Jesus made was that exorcisms and miracles could be done in His name even if they are disconnected from the Father's will (Matt. 7:21–23). Spectacular maybe, but not God-serving. People who act that way are lawless, not royal subjects. Don't search the list for their names; they will be told to depart.

I suspect we'd see more miracles if we focused less on them and more on the full benefits of being listed. Reveling in our identity as children of the King, enjoying His presence in every part of life—nothing beats it.

Let's Hear It For ——————

(Context: Matthew 23:1–36. Parallels: Mark 12:38–40; Luke 11:37–54; 20:45–47.)

The applause from the audience and the handshake from my headmaster made the boring speeches at a school Prize Day worth it. The award for my project about the Vikings was the only one I ever received in junior high school. (I was Mister Average, most of the time.) I rarely attended school functions; that year, my parents insisted. They were proud of me; I was proud of me. Most of all, standing in the spotlight, on a raised stage, with the headmaster in his academic gown, in front of a thousand adults and students—wow! I had not sought or expected it, but the attention felt good.

The delight in being noticed begins early in life. Young kids often seek attention. They can be loud, dramatic, and unashamed as they do. In time, most parents help them tone it down. But we all know a few people who can't stop bragging or talking about themselves. Generally though, as we mature, we refine our skills. Blatant exhibitionism gives way to the refined adult art of getting noticed while avoiding any suggestion that we are directing attention toward ourselves—and without gloating when we get it.

Jesus said the scribes and Pharisees liked attention. *"They do all their deeds to be noticed by men; for they broaden their phylacteries, and lengthen the tassels of their garments. And they love the place of honor at banquets, and the chief seats in the synagogues, and respectful greetings in the market places, and being called by men, Rabbi"* (Matt. 23:5–7). Using His other term for them, "hypocrites,"

Jesus described their behavior: sounding a trumpet ahead of themselves when they made donations; praying on the street corners to maximize visibility; wearing a special gloomy fasting-face (Matt. 6:1–18).

None of us want to be called pharisaical. Most of us easily avoid strict legalism. Hopefully, we don't hinder people as they search to know God, unlike the religious leaders (Matt. 23:13; Luke 11:52). However, we probably overlook their lesser-known sin of attention-seeking. We may even wonder if it is a sin.

It's certainly not Jesus' way. One challenge of reflecting on what it means to be like Jesus is that He talked so little about Himself that we have to notice what He didn't say and watch His actions. Jesus only mentioned two of His character traits, "I am gentle and humble in heart" (Matt. 11:29). He also said the Son of Man came to serve and be a sacrifice (Matt. 20:26–28). Jesus had audiences of thousands but He readily left them for solitude.[1] Jesus appealed to people not to make Him known, especially in the early days.[2] (They usually ignored His request.[3]) Most of the Gospel records consist of Jesus' teaching and miracles that focus on God as our Father, the kingdom, and on His other grand themes. It's clear that Jesus lived what He spoke. He floodlit the Father. His silence about Himself shows what a contrast He was to the religious leaders—a contrast to us, too!

We behave somewhere between the Pharisees and Jesus; our egos relish admiring audiences at least a bit. It's a subtle force altering the course of our lives, like misaligned steering on a car. We devise our plans and goals with some element of attention-seeking or self-promotion. Busy looks good, busier even better. Jesus was different. Even apparent fruitlessness didn't bother Him: He could let people walk away and accept it when few miracles happened. He never hurried to accomplish anything, so He was never frustrated by delays. See what happens next

---

1. Matt. 14:13, 23; John 6:15.

2. Matt. 16:20; Mark 5:43.

3. "He could not escape notice" (Mark 7:24). Similarly in Mark 1:43–45; 7:36; Luke 4:37. Publicity would be fine after the resurrection (Mark 9:9).

time you are rushing to polish off your latest project and something blemishes or derails it. If I'm focused on a task and someone interrupts me, I struggle to make quality time for them. Not so Jesus. Interruptions didn't irritate Him. You see, everyday life frequently presented opportunities for Him to accomplish what He came to do.

Jesus came not to be noticed but so that people would notice God—accurately. Everything Jesus did aimed to bring God glory and usually met people's needs (John 17:1–5). The two things worked together: miracles resolved practical problems, demonstrated God's fatherly care, and showed His glorious power. Perhaps those motives partly explain why He was willing to suffer. The shame and pain of His death were nothing compared to the freedom it won for people, the glory of resurrection, and the establishment of the kingdom. If only we could live free from our craving for attention, we could follow Jesus' way—blessing others and exalting God.

Can we ever be free? Perhaps not entirely. However, in humility, we can admit that being noticed is an inescapable drive and at the same time recognize that it hinders Christlikeness. That way, we can frequently check ourselves and ask for God's help. Trying to overcome any sin on our own might seem like attempting to get a grip on a wet bar of soap—the harder we squeeze, the more it slips from our grasp. Being honest with ourselves helps us focus better on serving others and glorifying God—just like Jesus did.

JESUS' HOPE

Did Jesus hope for anything? We find no mention of it in the Gospels. For me, hope has been an engine propelling me through life. I hope for flourishing relationships, fruitful projects, increased provision that frees my time, and exciting new adventures. Hopes like these carry me beyond the dutiful and mundane. After experiencing dashed hope, fresh hope starts me moving again. So, what are we to make of the silence about hope in Jesus' life? I suggest that this is another area in which Jesus, by example, calls us to live differently.

Perhaps Paul understood. From a prison cell, facing possible execution, Paul expressed an *"earnest expectation and hope, that I shall not be put to shame in anything, but that with all boldness, Christ shall even now, as always, be exalted in my body, whether by life or by death"* (Phil. 1:20). He added that to die and be with Jesus would be wonderful for him, but to remain and labor for the Philippian believers would be better.

Paul often talked of the hope of resurrection life based on faith in Jesus. It distinguished Jesus' followers.[1] Paul knew the resurrected existence would be glorious, the completion of adoption as God's children (Rom. 8:19–25; Col. 1:27). Peter and John also spoke of this future hope (1 Pet. 1:3–4, 13; 1 John 3:2–3). But Paul was clearly motivated by a present hope too: for the exaltation of Christ as He turned everything from shame to glory *in this life* (Phil. 1:20).

---

1. Acts 23:6; 24:15, 21; 26:6–8; 28:20; 1 Cor. 15:19; Tit. 1:2; 3:7.

Jesus' life fits the pattern of the two hopes. His future hope was not so much a hope as a memory and certainty—like knowing we're headed back to the family home for a wonderful reunion. He expressed the second hope in His unwavering determination to obey the will of His Father for His glory in the present (John 7:18).

There's a place for other hopes. Paul hoped to visit Rome on his way to Spain (Rom. 15:24), to stay in Corinth for a while (1 Cor. 16:7), and to spend time with Timothy in Ephesus (1 Tim. 3:14). Hopes like that can still spice up our lives, but they did not *drive* Jesus or Paul. The best driving engine in this life is the expectant hope that our days in God can be a string of encounters and opportunities for God's glory.

Setting Priorities

(Context: John 5:1–30.)

How often do you hear or use the statement, "Sorry, I'm too busy"? Sometimes it is a legitimate reason to say, "No," but often, it's a lame excuse. It would be more honest to admit that we have other priorities for our time. So, how do we decide our priorities and organize our schedules? Jesus had a simple plan; He evaluated everything according to God's will.

> *I say to you, the Son can do nothing of Himself, unless it is something He sees the Father doing; for whatever the Father does, these things the Son also does in like manner. . . . I can do nothing on My own initiative. As I hear, I judge; and My judgment is just, because I do not seek My own will, but the will of Him who sent Me.* (John 5:19, 30)

Jesus' way is a standard for us to aim at. We begin to learn Jesus' criteria for deciding priorities when we admit that whatever we do *of ourselves* amounts to nothing.[1] Only doing God's will has lasting value. Jesus' activities flowed from watching His Father at work and listening to His voice.

---

1. More about phrases like, "of myself," in the next piece.

"Isn't that rather idealistic?" you might ask. "What about my business, my screaming children, my sick mother, the tree that just crashed through the neighbor's roof? Do I have to pray before I help clean up the messes?"

Of course you don't. Jobs and family are part of God's will for most of us; they fit His purposes too. He knows there will be seasons when our time is stretched thin by unusual demands like illness, crises, or a traffic jam on the freeway. He can use us in those situations too. Also, God gave us brains and bodies that need refreshment and relaxation; movie nights and workouts have their place too. Jesus was in tune with His Father all the time; as life buffeted Him and people interrupted Him, He had ready responses.[2] Setting aside special times to seek God before the day's demands begin is a healthy habit. It helps us focus and makes distractions less likely. But let's develop the practice of alertness to the Father in everything we do. "Father, show me what you are doing right now" is a good prayer to repeat throughout the day.

Jesus was responsive to needs. However, sometimes He turned down requests. He never said, "I'm too busy"; He was direct. In essence, He pointed out that "God has another purpose for me" (Luke 4:42–43).

---

2. It's hard to count the interruptions, but about 10 percent of the incidents recorded in the Gospels involve interruptions that led to healings or teachings.

TAKING THE INITIATIVE

(Context: John 5:17–47; 10:1–21.)

Initiative is generally considered to be a good characteristic. We hear the encouragement, "take the initiative," or the admonition, "use your initiative." However, Jesus seems to have thought about it differently. Several times, John records Jesus' words using the Greek *emautou* (literally, "of myself") to convey the sense of taking the initiative. The pattern is interesting.

In most cases, Jesus referred to what He did not initiate. First, the works that He did: *"I can do nothing on my own initiative . . . I do not seek my own will, but the will of Him who sent me. If I alone bear witness of myself, my testimony is not true"* (John 5:30–31). He said the same about His message. He spoke what the Father taught (John 8:28; 12:49; 14:10). He did not come to earth *of Himself* (John 7:28–29; 8:42). The Holy Spirit behaves in the same way, speaking only what He hears (John 16:13).

What a different way of living! What humility! To many of us, it seems inconceivable that we would not pursue our own ideas. And is it possible to perceive the Father's directions so frequently and accurately that we can follow His leading through our entire lives? Yet that is how Jesus lived—allowing the Father to guide Him.

There is one important exception to the pattern, one way in which Jesus *did* take the initiative. Nonetheless, in this too Jesus fulfilled the Father's will.

For this reason the Father loves me, because I lay down my life that I may take it again. No one has taken it away from me, but I lay it down on my own initiative (emautou). *I have authority to lay it down, and I have authority to take it up again. This commandment I received from my Father.* (John 10:17–18)

Jesus allowed Himself to be killed. It had to be His choice because, when the Father prompts His children to do something, He never forces submission. The perfect sacrifice must be freely given. That's why He gave us the freedom to choose between our ways and His. It's up to us whether we live in a Christlike way.

ROADBLOCKS

(Context: Luke 9:51–56.)

How do you respond to setbacks or roadblocks? For me, it depends on the situation. If my project meets resistance, or a successful ministry appears to decline, I start to hear a little voice. It nags me about personal inadequacy or failure. It annoys me.

I understand anger as a secondary emotion springing from other emotions. If we are threatened, hurt, or feel wronged, we might become angry. The grief cycle that follows a loss often includes anger. Obstacles and disappointments can trigger a similar response. Blocked goals threaten our self-esteem, so we tend to fight the obstruction, fussing and fuming as we push against it.

Most often, anger is either part of an active attempt to bulldoze a roadblock, or it is a vengeful lashing out at whatever causes the frustration as if demolition will remove the pain. Some people turn their anger inwards, sabotaging their own life. Anger can even be self-destructive, a way to eliminate feelings of disappointment and hurt by deadening the feeler.

Jesus had a goal blocked one day. He was traveling to Jerusalem through Samaria. His logistical team had gone ahead to arrange for His visit to a certain village. They failed. Instead of holding a welcome party, the Samaritans drew curtains and bolted doors. Jews on their way to Jerusalem should keep right on walking. Jesus was unfazed. James and John were furious.

They said, "Lord, do You want us to command fire to come down from heaven and consume them?" But He turned and rebuked them, and said, "You do not know what kind of spirit you are of; for the Son of Man did not come to destroy men's lives, but to save them." And they went on to another village. (Luke 9:54–56)

How could Jesus stay so calm? I think the answer lies in the threefold perspective that Jesus had:

- He knew we can never force anyone to accept the King and His kingdom. If He had insisted on Samaria's hospitality, people would have harbored bitterness against Him. Anger does not accomplish the work of God; it's inconsistent with the ways of the Son of Man.[1] Often, I need to accept my powerlessness and hand things to God, trusting in His power to change them in His time.

- Jesus understood timing. In this case, Samaria could wait. Jesus would soon die and rise from the dead. Then He would ascend to the Father and send the Holy Spirit. In just a few short months, disciples would return to Samaria in the power of the Spirit, and a breakthrough would come.[2] Ministry reversals and roadblocks should drive us to God. As we wait on God, He will show us more about His timing and how He wants to accomplish His goals.

- Jerusalem was Jesus' priority. What seemed like a mountainous offense to the disciples was a tiny bump on Jesus' road. He would press on. Samaria was not His goal—Jerusalem was. Let's focus on the highest calling that God has given us rather than being distracted by lesser ones. Let's be willing for God to clarify our vision when it's a blurred version of His own.

---

1. James 1:20.

2. Acts 8:5–25.

THE SUNLIT TRAIL

(Context: John 11:1–44.)

Unless you're into extreme sports or pursue a career of hazardous work, you probably avoid danger. I dodged danger in a calculated way once. My wife and I had come to the end of a difficult year working in Mozambique. Problems had snowballed, and we needed to leave. By then, my nerves were frayed, and my sense of God's leading had evaporated, leaving me anxious about our journey home. At night, armed rebel forces and bandits controlled sections of the two-hundred-mile road from the coast up to Zimbabwe. Normally, we would feel safe driving it during the day. Not this time. My recent track record of failures made catastrophe seem inevitable. The potential for an attack inflamed the throbbing gash in my spirit like pepper. Unwilling to risk the drive, I insisted that we buy plane tickets.

You can imagine my horror at check-in. A dozen ticketed passengers had shown up to fly on a ten-seater aircraft. We were at the end of the line! It was a cruel prolonging of the misery that fed my whirling sense of doom and disaster. Our flight the next day added more drama when a thunder cloud loomed ahead and forced the pilot to dodge it. My poor nerves!

Perhaps Thomas felt a bit like me by the time Jesus announced that He was returning to Judea, where Lazarus lay deathly ill.

The disciples said to Him, "Rabbi, the Jews were just now seeking to stone You, and are You going there again?" (John 11:8)

They had recently eluded a stoning party; how could Jesus think of heading back to danger central? Thomas glumly concluded, with loyal but pessimistic resignation, "Let us also go, that we may die with Him" (John 11:16). But Jesus lived above the fog of gloom. What the disciples viewed as dangerous as a dark alley in gangland, Jesus saw as a bright path. He put it this way:

> *Are there not twelve hours in the day? If anyone walks in the day, he does not stumble, because he sees the light of this world. But if anyone walks in the night, he stumbles, because the light is not in him.* (John 11:9–10)

Jesus discounted the danger that the disciples dreaded; Bethany basked in metaphorical sunshine. For Jesus, any route the Father signposted was a safe, sunlit trail. His finely tuned sense of the Father's will and ways made all the difference. It had to; it would be scandalous if Jesus did not live out His own teaching about a Father who won't even let a sparrow crash-land outside of His will (Matt. 10:29–31).

His calm approach to life is evident at other times too: sleeping in a boat-swamping storm, crossing the lake to confront a legion of chain-busting demons, naming the hypocrisies of the religious leaders to their faces, evicting traders from the temple—all frightfully risky to us danger-dodgers. One time, He faced abandonment, too. In that, He was unconcerned because the presence of the Father outweighed the loss of human companions (John 16:32).

Only once did Jesus decline a dangerous dare. That was when the devil suggested He jump from the temple. The light of God's will never shone on that feat. The Father had not said it—the devil had (Matt. 4:5–7; Luke 4:9–12).

Ok, I can hear someone objecting. "Wait! Jesus was killed just a short time after raising Lazarus. The disciples were right." But think about Jesus' perspective on life and death. He did not deny physical suffering; His focus was on spiritual life. Jesus' death on the cross was a painful and costly sacrifice that looked as though

He had fallen flat on His face in the dark, but it led to the glory of resurrection. God's purposes intersected and were completed as Jesus obeyed.

There's only one way to avoid being sucked into a whirlpool of fearful pessimism like the one I experienced in Africa—always seek the will and ways of God. That means we must learn His general purposes and fine tune our inner ears to His specific leading. Then we must do what He shows us, trusting that He will be glorified through it, whatever it costs us.

WHEN AND HOW TO WEEP

(Context: John 11:1–44.)

Why do we weep? Doesn't it boil down to pain? When we are physically or emotionally hurt, tears are one response. But we weep at the traumas, tragedies, cruelties, and injustices that other people suffer too. Some tears flow so deep they never reach the surface.

The shortest verse in the Bible tells us that "Jesus wept" (John 11:35). But why would He? After all, a few days earlier, He had said that Lazarus' sickness would glorify God and that He was going to awaken him from sleep (John 11:4, 11, 23). Jesus was not weeping because He would never joke around with Lazarus over lunch again. So, what triggered His tears? They flowed after Martha and Mary both expressed regret that He had not been there to heal their brother (John 11:21, 32).

> *When Jesus therefore saw her weeping, and the Jews who came with her, weeping, He was deeply moved in spirit, and was troubled, and said, "Where have you laid him?" They said to Him, "Lord, come and see." Jesus wept. And so the Jews were saying, "Behold how He loved him!"* (John 11:33–36)

If Jesus was not mourning the permanent loss of a beloved friend, perhaps His tears flowed in sympathy with other mourners. That's possible, but I think there's more. The words John used to describe the event suggest Jesus was moved with indignation in His spirit and was agitated or troubled.[1] What followed was a quiet weeping rather than a wailing like the others.[2] The pain didn't devastate Him as it had the wailers; it saddened Him. And that suggests the focus of His emotions was on death and its effect on other people.

We read of Jesus' grief and other emotions elsewhere. He withdrew after John the Baptist's beheading (Matt. 14:13). Perhaps that sadness was tinged with contemplation of what would happen to Him in a few years—He was counting the cost.[3] He had compassion (or its equivalents, mercy and pity) in five situations that led to healings or other miracles.[4] That includes His compassion for the widow grieved by her son's death (Luke 7:13). Each time, the term *splanchnizomai* indicates that His vital organs were involved. In the Bible, those organs are understood to be the seat of our emotions.

Alongside compassion, the other moving forces behind miracles were faith and a desire for God's glory. It's no surprise that Jesus' greatest emotional response, His faith, and a stated desire for God's glory united in His greatest miracle. All three are mentioned in the story of Lazarus. The death of Lazarus cut deeper than anything else He encountered—Lazarus and his sisters were His friends. The tragedy plumbed the depth of Jesus' human emotions and activated His divine power most profoundly.

One tendency I have is to be content with *feeling* compassion for people, but failing to *act* on it. Jesus' emotions never blinded Him or smothered His responses. He sometimes showed anger and grief at hard hearts and legalistic opposition, but potential backlash never deterred Him from acting (Mark 3:1–5). Jesus' emotions overflowed and led to action regardless of the cost. Do ours?

---

1. John 11:33, 38.

2. The sisters and the Jews wept profusely (the Greek verb is *klaio*); Jesus wept quietly (*dakruo*).

3. The grief was there in Gethsemane (Matt. 26:37–38; Mark 14:34). Luke describes it as fervent prayer and bloody sweat (Luke 22:44).

4. *Splanchnizomai* is the word in Matthew 9:36 (no miracle in this case); 14:14; 15:32; 20:34; Mark 1:41; Luke 7:13.

It's likely that our emotions sink to depths of despair if we believe we are powerless in the face of pain. How do we respond when we encounter someone with more than a common illness? Do we simply speculate about the causes of that "incurable," "inoperable," "terminal" cancer? Perhaps our lack of qualifications or experience inhibits us. Do we shun the weird and the wicked? What about the mentally ill, houseless, or gender confused? Maybe we dismiss simple and common ailments as too trivial. Being like Jesus means moving from compassion to action, no matter what size the challenge seems to be.

We can prepare for challenges like these in general terms by prayer and study around the issues. To respond to individuals in their times of desperation we need to be tuned in to the Lord's specific leading.

When and How to Whip

(Context: John 2:13–22.[1] Parallels: Matthew 21:12–16; Mark 11:15–18; Luke 19:45–46.)

It's not always clear what Jesus felt when He confronted or exposed the religious leaders, which He frequently did. Mostly, He seemed to use gentle hints or pointed questions. The Gospel authors rarely tell us anything about His body language or tone of voice, but on one occasion they do:

> *[Jesus] found in the temple those who were selling oxen and sheep and doves, and the moneychangers seated. And He made a scourge of cords, and drove them all out of the temple, with the sheep and oxen; and He poured out the coins of the moneychangers, and overturned their tables; and to those who were selling the doves He said, "Take these things away; stop making My Father's house a house of merchandise." (John 2:14–16)*

Did His whip crack the air? Did it produce welts? Perhaps it was just an intimidating prop used to get people moving. The tables certainly crashed to the ground; coins clinked, bounced, and rolled. I bet the animals bleated and

---

1. John places the clearing of the temple near the start of Jesus' ministry. I have included it at this point in the book because the other Gospel writers have it during Jesus' final week. Of course, it may have happened twice.

bellowed as they bucked and cantered over the flagstones. No doubt, onlookers chuckled. All the drama and harsh words have the marks of a public display of anger. Had gentle Jesus, meek and mild, blown it this time?

Plenty of us feel guilt and shame when we blow it. Expressing anger is one of the hardest things for us to do well. It activates so many emotions, insecurities, and unpleasant memories that most people find it uncomfortable. Unless it is so habitual that we have ceased caring about hiding it, displays of anger remain private; Jesus' anger is printed in a bestseller! He never apologized or showed any shame. But did He continue to sense the presence of His Father during and after those confrontations? Most of us don't.

Here's the thing. We will never understand the anger of God until we understand His love. In so many of our experiences, anger and love are like oil and water—they don't mix. Love often simply means being nice, but it has more to do with godly attributes like truth and justice than warm feelings. Love seeks the best for everyone; it must be tough to do that. Pointing out error clearly without being demeaning is loving when it enables someone to change for the better. Fighting injustice and disease reflects God's caring heart and improves lives.

Jesus targeted such evils. Temple traders were exploiting people who came to worship: exorbitant exchange rates for temple shekels and inflated prices for sacrificial animals. So wrong! A house of prayer for all nations should be easily accessible (Mark 11:17). Even the disciples received His indignation when they tried to shoo children away (Mark 10:13–16). Religious leaders were attention seekers, we could say "glory seekers," robbing God (Isa. 42:8; 48:11; Matt. 6:1–18; 23:5). They allowed their trivial traditions to become obstacles to healing (Mark 3:1–5). They misrepresented God and hindered people from healthy relationships with Him (Matt. 23:13). Jesus confronted all these abuses, though rarely with overt anger.[2] He did share our fiercest emotion, but His anger was well tamed and

---

2. You might like to reflect on various other confrontations: challenging John the Baptist not to stumble (Luke 7:23); exposing the Jews' murderous intent by using questions (John 7:19, 20, 23); calling out the children of the devil (John 8:31–59); rebuking Peter (Matt. 16:21–23); correcting the disciples' thinking about greatness (Lk 22:24–30); naming abuse (John 18:19–23).

trained. Mostly, He chose clear, wise words and formed them into questions and comments that prodded people to rethink their behavior. Once, a whip cracked.

Perhaps Paul's exhortation to be angry without sinning (Eph. 4:26) provides our best bridge to being like Jesus. You see, it's the way and the why of anger that determine whether it's sinful. To love someone while carefully directing anger at their sin is fine. To tackle systemic evil or stand up for the vulnerable and downtrodden is loving. If it's aimed only at defending or avenging ourselves, it could easily stray into sinfulness. We need to learn to scrutinize the roots of our anger and then plan how to express it (if at all) before grabbing our whips.

Knowing Greatness

(Context: Matthew 20:20–28. Parallels: Mark 10:35–45; Luke 22:24–27.)

You know that the rulers of the Gentiles lord it over them, and their great men exercise authority over them. It is not so among you, but whoever wishes to become great among you shall be your servant, and whoever wishes to be first among you shall be your slave; just as the Son of Man did not come to be served, but to serve, and to give His life a ransom for many. (Matthew 20:25–28)

On the issue of greatness, we face another chasm of difference between Jesus' thinking and prevailing unspoken assumptions in our world. Jesus captured the difference well in His words. Leaders sometimes exert lordship, flaunt their authority, and parade their tokens of "greatness." "But," He said, "followers of mine show true greatness by serving."

Why the different mindsets? There are two reasons. First, an assumption runs through most cultures that menial roles and dirty jobs are for lesser people. We might treat serving people respectfully, tip them well, and even take an interest in their lives, but the bottom line is, if we're not in similar jobs, we don't believe we are like them. Second, low self-esteem feeds both insecurity and pride. We argue about and assert our "greatness" when it seems to be in question. Pride often compensates for a deep sense of weakness or emptiness.

A few days after Jesus' comments about greatness, He wrapped a towel around His waist, poured water into a basin, and made His disciples fidget awkwardly by washing their feet. The idea of a respected teacher and Lord bathing macho size 10–13s was as foreign to them as it is to us. Jesus was free to do so because He had an accurate self-image. He knew His place with the Father, where He had come from, and where He was going (John 13:3). Jesus' self-esteem was anchored in heaven's throne room. No child of a king needs to be concerned about greatness. Jesus knew who He was. He knew His greatness—serving couldn't change that.

Neither could being served. Yes, there were times when Jesus received service. Asking for a drink seemed natural to Him (John 4:7). Luke tells of women who supported Him (Luke 8:2–3). Mary anointed His feet with perfume (Luke 7:38; John 12:3). The disciples collected a colt and arranged the Passover meal (Luke 19:29–35; 22:8–13). Jesus was comfortable with their service; it made no difference to who He was. He was under no compulsion to always serve, as though it bettered Him somehow, and He had no illusion that others should always serve Him.

Jesus did not share the assumption that service roles are for lesser people, either. Christlike service has nothing to do with status or self-esteem. Its focus is on using ourselves, our gifts, and our resources to bless and benefit others.[1] Our Lord and Teacher washed feet not only as an example of the act of serving but also of the appropriateness of expending ourselves for others. His greatness was evident in the freedom that His security gave Him to serve or be served, whichever was appropriate at the time, and to meet needs with maximum effectiveness. Greatness serves.

Any low self-esteem in us can be corrected only by fully absorbing Jesus' good news. The good news is that everything we are and have comes from God, and we are going back to Him (John 13:3). We are the Father's adopted children in Jesus. When we know who we are in Christ and discover the freedom and joy of serving others or being served, the false assumption about lesser roles for lesser people withers.

---

1. We could say the same about being kind, generous, merciful, or helpful.

BETRAYAL

(Context: 2 Timothy 1:6–14. Parallels: Matthew 26:47–56; Mark 14:43–50; Luke 22:47–53; John 18:1–11.)

It was one of those weeks. First, a customer became awkward about paying his overdue bill. Then an appropriate comment that I had made in private was repeated to a third party. By the time I heard about it, it was completely distorted and made me sound bad—like the product of a game of Telephone. Finally, to round off the week, I experienced betrayal by a friend who had misunderstood me and interpreted my words as critical.

I felt beaten up, slapped down, torn apart, and pierced to the core. Instead of being my usual buoyant self, I wanted to crawl into a hole and sleep for a long time until the storm of accusations passed. Why on earth would God allow all this? I could handle the unpleasant customer, but the Christian friends . . . ! Surely God was as upset as I was.

It was then that I realized His plan. He was exposing my reactions to the betrayal and misunderstandings. I had withdrawn: "Don't smile at me; I have no smiles left to return." I had run a hot bathtub of self-pity, filled it with soothing bubbles, and slid as far into it as I could—to wallow. I had no care or energy for other people, especially if they needed something.

What a contrast to Jesus. While Judas' betraying kiss still glistened wet on Jesus' cheek, Jesus stepped in as peacemaker and healer. He healed a servant's severed ear after Peter had sliced it off. He stopped the foolish swordplay of the disciples and prevented a small massacre. He could have summoned an angel army instantly, but He chose to allow the Scriptures to be fulfilled.

That contrast highlights the difference between my fleshly reaction to life and the response of the Holy Spirit. Pierce my human side, and you will see retaliation or retreat. Betray, mock, flog, or crucify Jesus, and nothing but the fruit and power of the Spirit flow out. Spirit-love, -power, and -truth kept coming. He never missed a beat.

Realizing God's plan comforted me. If betrayal and false accusations are His way of getting me to make more room for the Holy Spirit, then I accept. How about you?

> *For God has not given us a spirit of timidity, but of power and love and discipline. Therefore do not be ashamed of the testimony of our Lord, or of me His prisoner; but join with me in suffering for the gospel according to the power of God. (2 Timothy 1:7–8)*

THE SOUND OF SILENCE

(Context: Isaiah 52:13–53:12.)

Silence is the most ambiguous communication. It can mean so many things—or nothing. Perhaps it is a slow and deep reflection. Maybe it's a stunned, awkward, or embarrassed silence.[1] Is the person quietly plotting? Is it a calm before a storm? Or is it a smug, unspoken, "I don't need to answer you; I know better"? How do people interpret your silences?

What do we make of the silences of Jesus? At His trial, Jesus gave brief and respectful answers to the chief priests and to Pilate's direct questions (Matt. 26:63–65; 27:11). King Herod failed to get any response, perhaps because he was looking for a sign, not justice (Luke 23:8–9). Jesus said nothing to counter the testimony of false witnesses (Matt. 26:59–63), nor to the accusations of the chief priests and elders (Matt. 27:12). Content to see the Father's will unfold, He behaved as Isaiah said He would.

> *He was oppressed and He was afflicted, yet He did not open His mouth; like a lamb that is led to slaughter, and like a sheep that is silent before its shearers, so He did not open His mouth. (Isaiah 53:7)*

Silence can force other people to think. Perhaps Jesus' accusers struggled with His lack of responses for that reason. When an innocent person says nothing, it

---

1. Mark 3:4; Luke 14:4; 20:26 are examples of awkward silences, Mark 9:34 of an embarrassed silence.

could be they have no defense. But Jesus was inviting the authorities to examine themselves. Theirs was an awkward silence with an uncomfortable conclusion—guilty judges.

The same thing happened when the scribes and Pharisees brought an adulteress as live bait for a trap to catch Jesus. After calling for the sinless ones to stone her, they heard no more than the gentle swish of a finger scratching in the dust (John 8:8).

What about that poor Canaanite woman with the demonized daughter? Jesus said nothing when she begged for mercy. Was it racial discrimination, a stony rejection, or something else (Matt. 15:21–23)? Could it be that the silence was Jesus' way of drawing out her faith? How far did she believe His merciful power would extend? How persistent would she be, especially when He compared her with a puppy dog? As we get to know God, we learn that He sometimes tests our faith in a similar way.

Knowing someone well helps us guess the meaning of their silence. Most likely, the meaning of a person's silence fits the pattern of their behavior under similar circumstances. From the person who is given to angry outbursts, silence is a billowing thunder cloud, or magma rising to the surface, ready to erupt. From the weak, fearful, or self-pitying, silence suggests an inner drizzle of tears. In Jesus, it is surely wisdom, love, gentle conviction of error, a challenge to greater faith, or a welcoming of the Father's will.

We should probably explain our silences. Those of us who are treading the path of Jesus to become more like Him still have a cloud of dust in our wake. People remember us for what we used to be like. They interpret our silences based on past behavior. It is hard for them to know when a silence is Christlike and when our old self is on a comeback. Jesus never sinned; His communication was always godly; no one ever needed to question the purity underlying His silences (1 Pet. 2:22–23). Considering how we can express our silences in words forces us to examine our hearts and welcome the conviction of the Spirit. How can my heart and my silences be more like Jesus'? When should I explain my ambiguity?

Stress Tests

(Context: Hebrews 2:9–18; 5:7–10.)

It was fitting for Him, for whom are all things, and through whom are all things, in bringing many sons to glory, to perfect the author of their salvation through sufferings. . . . Although He was a Son, He learned obedience from the things which He suffered. And having been made perfect, He became to all those who obey Him the source of eternal salvation. (Hebrews 2:10; 5:8–9)

What mysterious statements! Surely the author of our salvation did not need to be perfected or learn obedience; wasn't He perfect and obedient already? And weren't His sufferings just part of the crucifixion ordeal that was necessary to save us? Well, the writer of Hebrews reveals an additional purpose.

Suffering is, in essence, any undesirable circumstance in which we find ourselves. Our instinctive reaction is to want "out." We have no control over some kinds of suffering; unannounced, it can leap from our circumstances in the form of accident, illness, or disaster. But we sometimes expose ourselves to suffering by doing what's right. When obedience to God results in a measure of suffering, alternative options are always there to tempt us with easy pain relief. It seems crazy to decline the offer. Daniel and his friends risked their necks by rejecting Nebuchadnezzar's tasty menu and refusing to worship his image, or stop praying to God, as King Darius' advisors demanded (Dan. 1, 3, 6).

Rejecting ungodly indulgences brings another kind of suffering. It happened to Joseph when he bolted from the seductive lure dangled by Potiphar's wife (Gen. 39:1–20). Sin is always more desirable than self-denial. We deprive our pleasure-seeking instinct every time we resist fornication, adultery, theft, or any other sinful pleasure.

Both kinds of chosen suffering enhance the power of temptation. Jesus remained obedient to His Father, which meant resisting intense temptations and enduring suffering. Embracing the cross perfected His perfection by proving His obedience. Think of it this way. A newly constructed house can have every angle precise and not a nail bent or missing. The builder may proclaim that his work is perfect and ready for occupants. Nonetheless, the house must first pass inspections. When it comes to the plumbing, an inspector has to test the pipes under pressure to prove they function without leaking. Theoretical perfection becomes a reality by performing under pressure.

Like the house, Jesus was flawless; what He went through pressure-tested Him. Some tests were extreme. In Gethsemane, He could have opted to refuse the cup of God's wrath (Luke 22:42). Angel armies hovered alert for His summons to rescue Him from the cross; He declined to issue the order (Matt. 26:53). The cross was the ultimate test of obedience because it utterly defied the human, instinctive love of life and hatred of pain. Jesus remained sinless because He never stepped off the trail of God's will.

It's easy to zoom in on Jesus' last days and miss any application of stress testing to our own lives. But suffering (potential, imagined, or real) comes with faith challenges of every size, every call to obedience. Just because it's not as graphic and physically final as whips and nails doesn't mean the battle is not real. Sometimes we have to walk away from our people for a while to go where Jesus goes. We feel insecure turning down a stable salary and relying on God for provision when He calls us to that. The tests of Joseph and Daniel come to us in a thousand tiny versions. Does it count for much if we resemble Jesus only when we thrive and are in our element? To work Christlikeness into us thoroughly, testing is necessary (Rom. 5:4). So, instead of assuming we should fight every difficulty as an attacking enemy or as a throwback to the fall, we should ask whether it has a purpose.

Jesus faced all the tests we face; He's an example to us (Heb. 4:15). But He also broke the tempter's ultimate power—death (Heb. 2:14–15). We have nothing left to fear, and so, no reason to be held hostage by threats of suffering and death. And we're not lone weaklings; Jesus will help us pass every stress test (Heb. 2:18; 4:16). Every time we do, we become a little more like Him.

FOUR FINAL PRAYERS

(Context: Matt. 26:36–46; 27:34–50; Luke 23:33–49.
Parallels: Mark 14:32–42; 15:24–41; Luke 22:40–46; 23:44–46; John 19:17–37.)

Although we will never experience the intensity of Jesus' suffering, we sometimes find ourselves in situations that are similar in type. Jesus anticipated trouble: betrayal, abandonment by friends, false accusations, a mock trial without due process, unjust condemnation, jeering, torture, and a cruel death. We face lesser troubles. Perhaps socially acceptable curses fly easily from our mouths when someone cuts us off on the highway; Jesus' lack of words during those days is surprising, so His choice of four quick prayers is instructive.

- In Gethsemane, Jesus' experience of human tension is obvious. He asked to be spared God's crushing wrath, but He wrenched Himself back and surrendered to His will. *"My Father, if this cannot pass away unless I drink it, Thy will be done"* (Matt. 26:42). We need to come to terms with the relationship between suffering and obedience. Obeying God is hardest when it involves loss or pain. As we pay the price of obedience, we grow more like Jesus. His initial human wavering is exactly where we often find ourselves; His final resolve should be our goal.

- We catch the inner agony of Jesus' crucifixion in His cry, *"My God, My God, why hast Thou forsaken me?"* (Matt. 27:46).[1] More than all the

---

1. This is a quotation from Psalm 22:1.

emotional and physical pain evident in the bloody sweat of Gethsemane (Luke 22:44) was His sense of being severed from His Father. Feeling that God is not speaking or acting for even a short time is hard for us if we are used to His presence. If His apparent unresponsiveness continues, our feelings of abandonment intensify. Devilish accusations, which suggest we have committed some unknown sin, pierce us easily then. Doubts about God's existence flourish in dark places. It takes great faith to trust God in the silent times. However, the psalm Jesus quoted in His cry ends with praise; we can imagine Jesus reciting the remaining verses quietly and comfort rising with each stanza. The agony couldn't alter who He was, inside or out.

- *"Father, forgive them; for they do not know what they are doing"* (Luke 23:34). Instinct wants to lash out, to change, punish, or get even with those who hurt us. Jesus gave no place to those responses because He knew His opponents were only misguided players in God's bigger plan to open the door to His kingdom for anyone who chooses. The way of bargaining, bitterness, and unforgiveness is the way of the flesh; Jesus lived heaven's life. Many of us find it difficult to forgive others. Only by seeing ourselves and them in the context of God's bigger plan and our respective relationships with Him can we forgive as Jesus did. It's difficult to beat down love and forbearance in a child of God And it's hard to condemn spiritual orphans who don't know better because they don't know God.

- Jesus' dying words revisit His surrender in the garden but add blind faith—faith that something wonderful lies beyond the blackness. *"Father, into Thy hands I commit my spirit"* (Luke 23:46).[2] We want to prove our innocence, have the pain removed, or return everything to what it was. All those desires are understandable, but worthless com-

---

2. This is a quotation from Psalm 31:5, which is full of statements of trust and hope in God.

pared with trusting ourselves to the affirming resurrection of the Father. We can't dictate what resurrection will look like; we must be open to receive whatever God has planned, just as Jesus did.

For Jesus, anything other than these four prayers might have been an attempt to argue God out of His will. These four together highlight surrender amid human-inflicted suffering and even spiritual desolation. If you're like me, it's hard to trust God in new situations. I sometimes assume the outcome will disappoint—like some previous outcomes I have experienced—so I make a fuss. But with time I learn to trust and obey. In the past, I relied more on my human nature and less on God. Now, each new situation is an opportunity to exercise greater trust in God.

Jesus faced the ultimate unknown with maximum faith and received the greatest glory and vindication. What if we choose to surrender with the same confidence as Jesus? What if we focus on God's faithfulness to birth a glorious resurrection on the other side of pain and death? Surely we'll break through the forgiveness blockages, discover deeper peace, and be of more use to God.

Focused on Joy

(*Context: Hebrews 12:1–3.*)

When another driver does something stupid or dangerous, my expressions, though mild, come quickly. Injustice or abuse produces a more powerful reaction in most of us. So, have you ever wondered why Jesus said so little during His trials?

Faced with false accusers at the high priest's house, Jesus mostly kept quiet.[1] His answers to Pilate were short and simple.[2] Herod heard a disappointing silence.[3] Through all the scourging, mockery, and crucifixion, Jesus stayed almost silent. Could it be that He had something else on His mind? The writer of the book of Hebrews points to a joy:

> *Fixing our eyes on Jesus, the author and perfecter of faith, who for the joy set before Him endured the cross, despising the shame, and has sat down at the right hand of the throne of God.* (Hebrews 12:2)

This verse follows a long section about faith heroes. Jesus, the author and perfecter (or beginner and completer) of faith, is our prime example. The writer urges us to copy His faith more than anyone else's. So, knowing how Jesus exercised faith is essential. It's important to recognize that faith is not theoretical;

---

1. Matthew 26:57–68.

2. Matthew 27:11–14; John 19:9–12.

3. Luke 23:9.

it doesn't stop at what we know or have experienced. Faith always seems to lead to some kind of test or choice: will we align with what God says, even though it costs us something? Jesus faced the ultimate test with the highest price—shameful, unjust, agonizing death.

Confronted with an unfair, life-or-death trial, most of us would immediately fight back or try to dodge. Justified punishment is one thing, but shouldn't we defend ourselves against undeserved accusations? We doubt that there's any point in suffering unnecessarily; Jesus simply endured it.

Notice too that Jesus "despised" the shame of the cross. The Greek word, *kataphronesas*, can mean, "think little of." Evidently, a basic cost-benefit analysis went on in Jesus' mind. He weighed the joy set before Him against the price of the indignity and pain. Compared to future joy, the cross was nothing to fight against. Compared to that joy, His human life and dignity were not worth preserving.

Jesus could stay silent, like a sheep led to slaughter, because self-defense would have distracted Him from focusing on the joy. It's easy for us to rail against injustice, curse our enemies, groan and complain against pain, and beg God to end a travesty or to restore peace and happiness. Silence signals submission. Silence allows us to focus on the One we can trust with our unseen and seemingly impossible future.

So what joy did Jesus see ahead? We won't have a complete answer until we follow Him over that same horizon of obedience to the Father's will, regardless of the cost to us. But we do know that Jesus now sits with God. The presence of the heavenly Father is most precious. It's promised to us too. God dwells with those who love Him and keep His word (John 14:23). I am sure Jesus also glimpsed resurrection life for Himself and His followers. That's life in a new dimension, life unlimited by time or worldly concerns, life as part of the King's family, empowered to do His will.

MOVE 37

(Context: Mark 8:27–38. Parallels: Matthew 16:13–26; Luke 9:18–26.)

Go is probably the most complicated game in the world—simple to learn, extraordinarily difficult to master. Players take turns placing their black or white stones on a 19 × 19 board. The basic goal is to surround and capture the opponent's stones. With 10^{170} possible configurations of stones (more than the number of atoms in the universe) the complexity is astronomical.[1]

In March 2016, Lee Sedol, who held eighteen world *Go* titles, played a five-game match against Alpha Go, a powerful AI computer built and trained by Google's Deep Mind team. Alpha Go won 4–1. *Go* aficionados were shocked. The most memorable move was Alpha Go placing the thirty-seventh stone. No human master would have made such a move. It appeared to be a critical mistake at the time. Experts said the programming must be flawed. But with hindsight, they called it the turning point of the second game.

People often saw Jesus as a flawed leader. Many of His actions seemed like critical mistakes for someone who made veiled messianic claims. Critics would say, "Don't be humble—carefully preen and promote yourself. You mustn't befriend bad guys, touch lepers, silence fans after performing spectacular miracles, and turn down opportunities to become king. Only servants wash feet. Messiahs do none of those things."

---

1. That is 10 with 170 zeros after it. One billion is a mere 10^9.

Jesus' life culminated in something like a game-changing Move 37. The "move" was no accident. He was calculated and upfront about it. Peter was forceful when he rebuked Jesus, thinking Him foolish.

> *[Jesus] began to teach them that the Son of Man must suffer many things and be rejected by the elders and the chief priests and the scribes, and be killed, and after three days rise again. And He was stating the matter plainly. And Peter took Him aside and began to rebuke Him. But turning around and seeing His disciples, He rebuked Peter, and said, "Get behind me, Satan; for you are not setting your mind on God's interests, but man's."* (Mark 8:31–33)

A radical difference exists between the life of Christ and the life of the world. Christ knew that victory over the prince of the world could come only through suffering and death. The world rebukes such thinking, urging strong, positive attitudes to overcome every obstacle. Fallen human interests conflict with God's.

We must learn that each of us is thoroughly wrapped up in worldliness. Change is not as simple as installing a new program. Each step following the Master takes a careful choice and a huge effort to overcome the inertia. So much inside us cries out to be preserved from pain and death; yet so much the Lord calls us to requires facing some pain. But, each step in the right direction, although it feels like defeat to our human nature, is another spiritual victory. Every time we rebuke that complaining and cautioning inner voice, we loosen the wrappings a little more.

Victory in God's kingdom comes when least expected, in apparent foolishness and weakness (1 Cor. 1:26–29), through humility, or after a painful death. Jesus went there. He shocked Satan. If you want to experience real victory, learn and live this kingdom principle.

Few things are as marvelous as watching a seed buried in chilled, sodden soil, sprout, bloom, and bear fruit (John 12:24).

THE THIRD SON

(Context: Luke 15:11–32.)

Years ago, when fans bought the latest songs on vinyl records, which they played on turntables, "singles" had two sides—A and B. Record companies put the song they expected to sell best on side A. However, a side B tune occasionally surprised them and hit the charts.

As I read the story of the father and his two sons in Luke chapter fifteen, I can't help imagining that Jesus had a chart-topping B side to the parable playing in His mind. He experienced a beautiful resolution of all the jarring arrhythmias and discordant notes of the version we are familiar with. His was a ballad of the harmonious life of the father with a third son.

The third son is thoroughly present with his father. His thoughts never wander to imaginary lands, scouting a path for his feet to follow. Yellow brick roads can't excite him; he knows they're clay, not gold, and that such roads peter out long before reaching any meaningful destination. Loose living has no appeal for him; forbidden fruits are never worth picking when you live in an Eden. The best life is with the father; home is straightforward and reliable, but never boring. He values it so highly that no one could ever tempt him away with fake promises of fame and fortune. Many children cut short their times with the father as though the next task is more important; the third son lingers.

He's not just present in body, either; he's with his father in every way. He has no need to be task-centered, thinking to earn praise and reward—he needs no ego boosters. He doesn't want to work on his own; he doesn't need the recognition and credit that solo accomplishments can bring. To dream up tasks independently or modify his assignments would rob him of the delight of doing the father's explicit will. The dull life of a dutiful son would be servitude to him. That existence can only satisfy someone who thinks they can control the father's pleasure and their own reputation—someone who is outwardly admirable but inwardly empty and lonely.

For him, being present means being completely in tune with the father. He feels his father's grief over lost brothers and sisters, and his sadness as he watches other kids slaving alone for long hours in the distant fields. He shares the father's joy whenever wanderers realize what they are missing and return to the healthy life.

Life with the father is best. They do everything as partners—he's the junior, watching and following the father's lead. Work goes so smoothly that every day feels as restful as a Sabbath. This son lacks nothing. He dresses in the rich robes that distinguish the leading family. He can stand tall, or saunter in the best sandals. He wears the father's ring of authority and shares in his wealth. The third son would never dream of taking a mere portion of the father's estate when he can dip into his inexhaustible supply at any time. Everything that the father has is his to share in (Luke 15:31). Out of his plenty and generosity, the father gives good things to his children (Matt. 7:11). The son eats what he wants, when he wants; celebrations are frequent when life is so abundant. His two brothers come on the occasions when they need something from their father; the third son enjoys him all the time.

His is no clingy relationship marred by a fear of losing some of the father's attention and resources to competing siblings. The third son delights to share the father with an expanding family of brothers and sisters.

And so, Jesus invites us all to become like Him, to join in His song.

ABOUT THE AUTHOR

John Avery is the author of *The Name Quest: Explore the Names of God to Grow in Faith and Get to Know Him Better* (Morgan James Publishing, 2015). *The Name Quest* won the 2016 Oregon Christian Writers' Cascade Award for nonfiction. A compilation of short pieces, *The Questions of Jesus*, was published in 2022 followed by *The Kingdom of God* in 2023.

John is a trained teacher with over forty years' experience as a Bible teaching pastor, small group leader, missionary, and disciple maker. He has lived in England, Israel, Africa, and the Caribbean, ministering with Youth With A Mission (YWAM), an international student ministry, and local churches. He and his wife, Janet, now make their home in Oregon. John likes to hike, snowshoe, and cross-country ski. John writes short, thought-provoking Bible devotionals at www.BibleMaturity.com many of which will be compiled into books like this one. He maintains a comprehensive resource for all the names of God at www.NamesForGod.net.

Additional Resources

Available from major booksellers worldwide.
  ISBN: 978-1-63047-159-0

Collections of Two-Page Bible Devotionals

Watch for other compilations in the Sparks Series in titles or on topics like:

The Questions of Jesus (Published October 2022)

The Kingdom of God (Published March 2023)

Our Identity as Children of God

Talking to God

Faith in God

The Spirit of God

Following the Voice of God

Revival from God

Prophets of God

Names of God

Followers of Jesus

Kings of Israel (David, Saul, and others)

Fathers of Faith (Abraham, Jacob, and Moses)

Various other in-depth devotionals are at www.BibleMaturity.com.

9 798989 745203